THE EFFECTIVE
COMMUNICATOR

THE EFFECTIVE COMMUNICATOR

JOHN ADAIR

JAICO PUBLISHING HOUSE
Ahmedabad Bangalore Bhopal Chennai
Delhi Hyderabad Kolkata Mumbai

Published by Jaico Publishing House
A-2, Jash Chambers, Sir Phirozshah Mehta Road
Fort, Mumbai - 400 001
jaicopub@jaicobooks.com
www.jaicobooks.com

Printed in arrangement with
The Industrial Society
Robert Hyde House, 48, Bryanston Square
London W1H 7LN

THE EFFECTIVE COMMUNICATOR
ISBN 81-7224-428-2

First Jaico Impression: 1995
Fourth Jaico Impression: 2005

Printed by
Gayatri Enterprise
G-179, Sector-63, Noida.

CONTENTS

INTRODUCTION

This book is a practical guide to a key aspect of effective management — communication. It sets out clearly the systems required in organisations today — such as team briefing, upward consultation and quality circles — together with guidelines on how to set them up and sustain them over a period of time. In this field I have drawn freely upon the wealth of experience garnered by The Industrial Society.

But systems are only half the story. The other half is concerned with the attitudes and skills of those who operate them. The skills of speaking, listening, writing and reading are obviously important. Take speaking as an example. You do not have to be an orator or a witty after-dinner speaker, but you do have to be able to speak clearly, simply, vividly and concisely. For the communicative manager is not over-talkative: he or she knows when and how to listen. Attitudes are the foundations of good communication. Your company's attitudes to people will largely determine the value it places on communication, and whether or not it is willing to invest in establishing the proper systems and the training of managers and supervisors to become effective leaders. It has been wisely said that 'he who communicates is he who leads'.

In the first chapter we shall explore the manager's responsibility for communication — why it matters and what should be communicated — and briefly survey the various methods. The crucial importance of face-to-face, two-way communication for vital information about the common task, the team and matters which affect each individual has become absolutely clear from research done on the subject. Therefore Chapters 2 and 3 focus on team briefing and consultation, the two principal systems for 'downward' and 'upward' communication.

Within the 'human side of enterprise' I have always believed that there are three major concepts — (a) leadership, (b) communication and (c) decision making, problem solving and creative thinking — which overlap considerably. When you listen, for example, you are doing all three — meeting individual needs, communicating and receiving new ideas. Therefore Chapter 4 on quality circles and suggestion schemes is as much about problem solving and creative thinking as about communication. It shows you how good communication — both systems and leadership ability — can help you to harvest the ideas and suggestions of everyone who works for the company. Today we are all in 'people businesses'. Remember that everyone who works with you has 10,000 million brain cells!

Communicating by paper — both writing and reading — is an inescapable part of any manager's job. Chapter 5 presents a simple three-point programme for effective report writing, while Chapter 6 surveys the role of house journals and other forms of written communication within organisations.

The skills of managing communication in meetings as well as talking/listening effectively yourself are the subject of Chapter 7. It reminds us that it is not the quantity but the quality of meetings that matters. Discipline yourself to start them and end them on time. Within that shared time framework you should deploy the skills of chairmanship to ensure that the objects of the meeting are achieved and decisions duly recorded.

Of course communication is not all 'inside the egg' of the organisation. We have to communicate effectively with the all-important customer, as well as many others who impinge upon our daily work. Guidance on the art of letter writing and how to practise the key skills of using the telephone is set out in Chapter 8. Lastly, the kind of communication required to establish real teamwork in the office is described in Chapter 9. Communication, like charity, should begin at home — with those who are working closest to you.

I hope that you will enjoy this book as well as finding it instructive. Good communication should be fun. It helps people to enjoy their work — even in difficult and challenging times — as well as to gain financial benefit from it. It is your long-term investment in people and it will pay handsome dividends over the years.

I suggest that you read it with pencil and paper at hand, making notes on 'action points' — things that you can take action on yourself — in order to improve your own communication skills or to bring about changes in your company along the lines I advocate in this book. Good luck!

/ THE MANAGER'S RESPONSIBILITY FOR COMMUNICATION

The success of managers depends, primarily, on their ability to communicate, to all the people for whom they are responsible, first what they need to do and second the importance of doing it. If you are to be a successful manager, you must also encourage communication in the reverse direction, so that you can harness the ideas, views and experiences of the people who are actually carrying out the job.

Why does communication matter?

Communication matters for a plethora of reasons.

First, communication failures are costly. For example, in one large organisation it was discovered that, out of thirty-five stoppages, no fewer than eighteen were due to failures in communication. The cost of these stoppages could not be measured merely in terms of the hours lost: they upset the whole rhythm of production, lessened cooperation between employees and their managers, and created ill-feeling, which always reduces productivity.

Second, during times of change within an organisation, the full benefits of the change can be achieved only where there is an adequate communication system for explaining directly, preferably face-to-face, to the employees what is required of them and why.

Third, adequate communication results in greater productivity, because employees direct their work more effectively and cooperate more with their leaders. One City organisation has actually monitored staff productivity and found that there is a significant upsurge after each monthly briefing by management.

Fourth, you may find that executives of good potential are leaving your organisation simply because they are unaware of their prospects. Finding and training a successor from outside

1

the organisation is a costly matter, and it lowers morale among colleagues. In order to avoid such situations, you need to communicate to your subordinates what you think of them and what their futures within the organisation are likely to be.

Fifth — and this cannot be stressed too often — there is no monopoly of wisdom at the top of organisations. You simply cannot afford to waste the ideas and inventiveness of your subordinates. You need to set up a communication system such that you receive every 'good idea' produced by an employee: by the law of averages, many of these will be useless, but the remainder will vastly increase your organisation's profits and/or make it possible for you and your staff to take life a little easier. A good example was provided quite a number of years ago when the staff of one company were asked to produce suggestions for increasing efficiency. An employee proposed that, by using a proprietary oven-cleaner on production surfaces, productivity could be substantially improved. When asked why he had not made this suggestion before. he replied that management had never before given the slightest indication that they wanted to hear the views of the workers. He had been working for that company for *thirty years!*

Sixth, people will give of their best to their work only if they fully understand the decisions that affect them and the reasons behind those decisions. Our subordinates need to understand what they have to do and why, how they are performing against the budgets and the targets they have been set, and what their conditions of employment are. Given this understanding, our employees can become *involved* in what they are doing, so that we enjoy greater efficiency, higher morale, and improved cooperation.

Finally, would you be happy working if you did not know why you were doing your work? No, obviously not. So clearly you owe it to your staff to make sure that they are not in that situation.

Communication, to be effective, cannot be a haphazard process. In this book we shall look at the various systems and techniques whereby communication between you and your staff can be improved — so that everyone is better off.

What should I communicate?

The first thing to decide is: What are your priorities? The system of communication you use will depend on your answer to this question. Clearly you cannot tell everybody everything, or consult everybody about everything, because if you did you would never get any work done.

The old idea was that you told your subordinates what you thought would interest them, skipping all the boring stuff. But this is not really good enough. If you operate this principle, you find that you are not only missing out many things which it is important that your subordinates understand, you are also telling them a lot of things which, while perhaps interesting, are of little relevance. Of course, it is more difficult to get across things to employees which they find essentially uninteresting, but nevertheless you should persevere, and make sure the points are fully understood.

This matter of *understanding* is important. It is the vital first step in ensuring that your consultations (see Chapter 3) with your employees are successful. Too often, managers seek ideas and opinions in formal consultation structures without having first given their employees sufficient understanding of their work for realistic ideas and opinions to be generated. Moreover, people will go along with a decision with which they profoundly disagree just so long as they understand why it has been taken. If they don't, you are very likely to find yourself with a revolt on your hands.

The primary things that need to be communicated to people come under two headings: matters that affect their job, and matters that affect their employment. Under the first heading come all the things that will enable them to do their job better; under the second come all the things concerning their rewards for having done the job. It is vital — as much for the good of the organisation as for the good of the individual employee — that such matters be communicated effectively.

And doing so is an important part of your job.

Which method do I choose?

The worst communication method you can use is the grapevine. To be true, the grapevine can be useful, but you use it at your peril. Facts can be communicated accurately through the grapevine — and very swiftly: sometimes, for example, the news about a forthcoming appointment can be communicated before the formal decision has been made! The great disadvantage is that the grapevine always gives an *uncharitable* reason for any decision, and that is obviously bad for employee cooperation. The grapevine will say that someone has been promoted because she is about to marry the boss's son, not because she is good at her job; and all the people who are not being promoted will feel (quite naturally) resentful. So you owe it to yourself, your organisation and your employees to make sure that there is some systematic way whereby your subordinates can learn about the things that matter.

There are three main ways in which you can communicate effectively:

- through face-to-face communication with your employees (see Chapters 2 and 7)
- through discussing matters with staff representatives (see Chapter 3)
- through 'mass methods', such as a house journal or the organisation's notice-board (see Chapter 6)

You have to decide which method to use, and to be clear about what can be communicated through each of them and what the limitations of each of them are. All too often, communication breakdowns occur because managers are using the wrong methods or because they are trying to communicate the wrong type of information through a particular system.

Face-to-face communication between managers or supervisors and their employees is good in many ways. Part of the job of being a leader is to be the person to whom people look for explanations about the things that matter to them, and so, by becoming the direct communicator, you become a more effective leader. Moreover, you are in fact the best person to act as communicator, because the things happening within the organisation that will be most · important to your subordinates will arise from management decisions (or management/union decisions) — you know exactly *why* something is being done, and your employees will benefit from getting the news straight from the horse's mouth. You can tailor your explanation according to the interests of the particular group you are addressing, and then you can answer any questions that are forthcoming — something that is vital if your employees are to understand what is going on. Finally, face-to-face communication saves a lot of time, ensures common understanding, and is the most powerful method of 'selling' ideas and building group commitment.

All of which might make you wonder why we bother even considering the other techniques of communication. However, the face-to-face approach has some weaknesses. For example, it can be very expensive in terms of management time and, if there are more than two levels of communication between senior management and the front line, it can be a total fiasco unless properly organised — which means that *you* have to spend time and effort doing the organising. Another consequence of there being several levels of communication is that the hierarchy of leadership cannot by itself adequately cope with *upward* communication: senior management is often quite unaware of the strength of feeling at the bottom, because what has been reported to them has been diluted by passing through the various levels.

Communication through representatives has many advantages, because you can explain a policy directly to a few of the employees concerned, and discuss it with them; clearly this is more economical of your time and effort than setting up a system of levels of management explaining the policy to every single employee. Also, representatives will tell you in forthright fashion exactly what the feelings are on the shop floor or in the typing pool, and the formal contacts made through meetings with representatives lead to more informal contacts, something which cannot help but be good for efficiency. However, although the representatives will usually understand your message completely, they will very often fail to pass it on accurately to the other employees — particularly in the case of unpleasant decisions. This is because the representatives are being put in the invidious position of being management mouthpieces: this is not their job, and if you force them to do it you are making both yourself and them look shoddy.

What, then, of mass methods? Notice-boards, house journals, managers' newsletters, booklets, circulars, mass meetings — these offer the cheapest ways of giving information to large numbers of people, and they allow it to be done quickly. They are a necessary aid to communication from management. But, like the other techniques of communication, they have their problems. For example, while one of the strengths of a house journal or a notice on the board is that you can ensure that the information you are transmitting is absolutely accurate, you have no way of knowing that it is being *received* accurately. Your employees cannot ask a notice-board or a circular a question, and so they may completely misunderstand what you are trying to communicate (a factor exacerbated by the grapevine). Likewise, although in theory people can ask questions at mass meetings, in practice most of us will be too shy to do so at any meeting where there are more than twenty people present. Another important point is that mass means of communication can, by their very nature, cover only general aspects: what people *really* want to know is how they or their immediate working group are likely to be affected.

This matter of allowing for questions should be stressed. It is the only way by which you can ensure that everybody *understands* what is going on. There is a colossal difference between providing accurate information and getting people truly to understand that information. Experience has shown that, whatever other communication system you use, face-to-face encounters are vital, so that people can ask questions. Interestingly, explanation to a small group is better (as well as less time-consuming!) than to individuals: in a group, people benefit from hearing the answers to other people's questions and, of course, timid people profit through the fact that other people will ask the questions that they are too shy to ask.

Whatever technique of communication you choose for a specific situation, bear in mind that *any* systematic method is better than none at all. Obviously, the mass methods are easiest to use, and the face-to-face ones, through managers and supervisors, the most difficult. But, in a large organisation, communication both upward and downward will be unsuccessful unless you make judicious use of each of these three types of techniques.

Effective communication through managers and supervisors

The busier your working life, the more important it is that you have mastered a systematic communication drill. You cannot afford to hope that communication will simply 'happen' in some kind of casual or *ad hoc* fashion. For example, you might explain some change with brilliant lucidity to your immediate subordinates but then, by the time the information has passed down the ladder of responsibility, find that your message has become utterly garbled. Even if it has not, what almost certainly *will* happen is that the people in the front line will conclude that the change will come about solely because 'They' have decided that it will, or that it was all a 'management decision'. You could hardly concoct a better way of ensuring that your employees are disgruntled.

Of course, because 'They' have given the order, your employees will almost certainly do what is required, but they will not actively *cooperate*. And the difference between sullen obedience and constructive cooperation is very often the difference between loss and profit. If all you can get is obedience, then you are not doing your job as a manager.

If downward communication through line management is to be effective then it has to be systematic. The object is to ensure that all employees have the decisions that affect their jobs or their conditions of employment fully spelled out to them, face-to-face, by their immediate boss. In order that this may come about, there are two things you must do: first, you must establish a team-briefing drill that ensures communication, *via* supervisors, right down the line to the work group; and, second, you must make certain that all the necessary information is known to your subordinate managers or supervisors.

Team briefing is a topic to which we shall return in the next chapter; here let us look at the task of ensuring that your subordinate managers know what they are talking about. The first thing to note is that information (especially about personnel policies) must be fed into the line of leadership accurately and speedily.

You will need a management bulletin which can be distributed at a few hours' notice according to a prearranged distribution list to each manager and supervisor whenever some decision affecting large numbers of employees has been taken. This bulletin should state briefly what has been decided and the main reasons for the decision — for example, details of trade-union settlements, changes in a staff job, or the introduction of a new way of working.

Every manager and supervisor should receive his or her own copy of the management bulletin, and certainly should not just be placed on a circulation list: circulation lists are notorious for the amount of time they require before the last person on the list sees the relevant bulletin — if ever. Do not cheapskate on the number of copies you produce of your management bulletins: it is a false economy to restrict the circulation.

The bulletin should also state whether or not the information contained in it should be communicated further. If so, you should spell out clearly *how* you want the information passed on.

A final point about management bulletins is that only urgent matters should be discussed in them. Otherwise, the bulletin gets put to the bottom of the in-tray, and possibly never emerges.

Mass methods

Of all the mass methods of communication, the most noteworthy are the following: the notice-board, house journals, managers' newsletters, accountability charts, employee handbooks, loudspeaker systems, phone-in arrangements, mass meetings, and annual reports. Let us look at these in turn.

First, *notice-boards*. The siting of these is important: not only should they be where people will see them, but they should also be positioned such that people can actually stop to look at them. At each site there should either be two notice-boards or one notice-board overtly divided into two parts: one section can be used for new and/or urgent notices and the other for less urgent (but nevertheless important) matters. Once a notice has been in the 'urgent' section for forty-eight hours it should either be moved over, if it is important, or thrown away, if it is not. All notices on the board should be signed by an individual — otherwise the employees are likely to feel that they are part of nothing more than an impersonal web — and a particular individual (preferably the departmental supervisor) should be put in charge of each notice-board. A final point to note is that, when you are composing a notice for the board, you should think about how you would express the information were you actually *speaking* to the people, face-to-face. Write down what you would say rather than mess around with literary elegance. People respond far more readily if, as they read the message, they can 'hear your voice'.

The main purposes of *house journals* — company magazines, company newspapers, call them what you will — should be to provide a mass means of explaining your organisation's activities and policies to the employees, to help the employees feel that they are involved in the organisation, and to create an atmosphere in which change is accepted. When you budget and plan a house journal you should be thinking in terms of frequency and flexibility. A cyclostyled journal may not look like much, but it is far more topical than a glossy magazine that is always a couple of months out-of-date because of printing schedules. Newsletters produced in this way should of course be distributed free to every employee; if you want to produce a glossy magazine as well, you can have it sent to each employee's home and you can make a nominal charge for it. Bear in mind, though, that people will resent even a nominal charge if they feel they are *obliged* to pay it for a magazine they may never read.

The contents of a house journal should be regarded as being in three thirds: one third should be devoted to product and other news that affects employees' jobs; one third to developments or changes in conditions of employment; and one third to social events and ephemera. Of course, news that might affect jobs should already have been communicated, *via* managers and supervisors, to those directly concerned; but repetition here is useful to inform those who are concerned, but less directly. The ephemera should not be regarded as an optional extra. One publishing company discovered that very few employees ever read its weekly newsletter until it began to contain jokey reports of the antics of the company cricket team: suddenly everybody, whether interested in cricket or not, turned to the column hoping for a good joke, and ended up reading the rest of the newsletter.

You can use your house journal as a way of communicating with clients, but generally speaking it is better to have a separate publication for this purpose.

We shall come back to the subject of house journals in Chapter 6. Here, however, we can note also the *manager's newsletter.* This can be regarded as a company newsletter that applies to, and is distributed to, the employees of only a single part of the organisation; it is, of course, prepared by the relevant manager or supervisor. Such newsletters should appear at least monthly, and preferably more frequently than that: whenever there is something important that employees might misunderstand what is going on. And do not try to economise by running off too few copies: unless every employee has his or her own copy, the whole exercise is a waste of your time.

Accountability charts are very useful. People must know who is their own direct boss, and who is their boss's boss. Every person should have a copy of a chart showing the ladder of responsibility.

Each employee should have also an *employee handbook* setting out the main rules and arrangements that apply to them. The handbook should be as brief as possible. If need be, it can be supplemented by booklets dealing with specific subjects — for example, disputes procedures. The best way of presenting the information in employee handbooks is usually in question-and-answer form, explaining specific aspects of conditions of employment. For example, it may be obligatory to provide employees with the rules of the pension fund in their full legal rigour. However, the resulting document will be comprehensible only to a fully fledged lawyer, and so it makes a lot of sense to give employees a question-and-answer version, written without jargon, which they can actually understand.

Loudspeaker systems tend to be used too frequently. They are unsatisfactory for putting over a policy, as the listener cannot even see the person speaking — let alone ask a question. So, unless you feel you really need it, drop your loudspeaker in a bucket of water at the earliest possible opportunity. Likewise, while *mass meetings* have a certain value — they are often the only chance employees get to hear senior management directly — they are a poor means of ensuring that employees gain any understanding of what is going on, because questions are impossible. Team briefing, working down the line, is a much more effective alternative.

Phone-in arrangements are used in a few organisations. The idea is that any employee can dial an internal number and listen to a prerecorded message discussing current activities, the reasons behind the company news, and so forth. Alternatively, the employee may be able to record a question, the answer to which will be conveyed later.

The publication of the *annual report* gives you a major opportunity to help your people understand the vital importance of their work. The annual report enables you to explain that, during the year, the people in the organisation have together done five different things:

● they have produced a certain volume of goods and services for other people
● they have generated the incomes of everyone employed by the organisation
● they have generated tax revenue which will pay for schools, hospitals, and so on

- they have enabled the company to put money aside for investment in future development
- finally, they have created a return on people's savings, through distributed profits.

Annual reports can also include information directly related to employees — for instance, safety and absenteeism statistics. Such data are particularly relevant if figures are compared from region to region or from department to department. Certainly, the figures should be complemented by comparisons and comments: the usual reaction to bald figures is an apathetic 'so what?'. Make it clear whether or not you are pleased with the figures, and explain why the results are better or worse than expected.

The effectiveness of the annual employee report depends upon how well it is distributed. Experience suggests that it is best distributed in a briefing or before a mass meeting. Many organisations mail the reports to their employees' home addresses. However your organisation goes about it, make sure that every employee does actually receive a copy of the report — and try to ensure that opportunites are available for the employees to ask questions and to discuss the information in the report with their colleagues. Otherwise, you are simply not communicating effectively.

Customer complaints

So far we have talked only about communication within the organisation. Towards the end of this book we shall discuss communication with people outside the organisation, but it seems sensible here to light briefly on the subject of customer complaints.

The most difficult situation in the field of customer relations is when something has gone wrong — the product has failed, promises have not been kept, deadlines have not been met — whatever the reason, the customer is quite rightly displeased, and it is up to us to deal with their displeasure.

It is quite understandable to want to go on the defensive — but it is also a big mistake. There is no surer way of losing a customer forever than to respond with something like: 'Well, no one's ever complained before.' You are implying that the customer is a pest and a fool, and, curious as it may seem, customers are not generally thrilled by this.

Oddly enough, it is actually more efficient to *encourage* customer complaints. They are a marvellous tool, providing more useful information about our products, services or performances than any number of surveys or praise-packed letters. If you use them correctly, complaints can work for you. Some researches have shown that if you merely encourage complaints — for example, by having an accessible and publicised customer relations or complaints department — you can increase customer-retention by as much as 10 per cent. If you go one stage further, and are seen actually to *do* something about the complaints you receive — following them up and reporting back to the customer — your rate of customer-retention increases by a staggering 70 per cent. But if you pursue the complaints and come to a happy compromise with the customer, the rate goes up by no less than 90 per cent!

By contrast, discouraging or rejecting complaints is bad policy. The same researches showed that, when customers found that their complaints were discouraged or that nothing was done about them, they told between 9 and 13 other people about the bad experience they had had; it is, after all, a natural human activity to gossip about the appalling treatment we have had at the hands of one company or another. This means that, by failing to communicate with customers who have complaints, you are not only losing those customers forever, you are ensuring that many more potential clients would not touch your company or its products with a bargepole.

But there is more to it than that. Not only do dissatisfied customers tell the world about your organisation's shortcomings, they fail to tell *you* the reasons for their dissatisfaction. Unless you know why they are unhappy, you will never find out why it is that you are losing customers — those customers who for one reason or another do not make a formal complaint, but simply cease trading with you.

It's therefore a vital aspect of communication to make sure that you listen to complaints and that you do something about them. Moreover, you must make sure that all your subordinates have the same idea drummed into them. It is useless your being receptive to criticism if the person on the switchboard is telling all complainants to get lost.

Is communication working?

In these participative days, a key factor in effective leadership is the extent to which you pay serious attention to communication, both upward and downward. The more trouble you take over communication, the better your people will work for you. If you take action to improve communication, you will find — like thousands of managers before you — that efficiency increases, 'as if by magic'. Except that there is no magic involved: all you have done is allow your subordinates to get more out of their jobs — and hence more out of life.

As with all other aspects of leadership, it is necessary to check that your communication is actually working.

'Walking the job' is an effective technique. Every now and then (and it is worth booking the time in your diary, as otherwise the 'mañana factor' comes into force!), simply walk around the place, chatting with the employees about their work, the weather, or anything else, and above all *listening* to what they have to say. You may be surprised by what you hear. If someone does not know why they are doing a particular job, or why a change has been made, then that means your communication system has broken down, somewhere along the line. For the short term, you should take the matter up with the person's immediate boss; but for the longer term you should take a pretty close look at your systems of communication.

Another, more formal, means of checking things out is through the use of questionnaires. There are two main types. In one, employees are simply asked how they heard about certain changes or decisions; their responses tell you how much is being communicated through your systems and how much is being bruited about via the grapevine. The other useful type of questionnaire is the 'attitude survey', in which employees are asked — with guaranteed anonymity! — what they know about various organisational policies, what their attitudes are to the organisation and their bosses, what they think about their employment conditions, and so on. You might find it worth employing an outside company to do this sort of survey, as often your employees will be reluctant to say what they really think if they feel there is a chance their remarks might be traced back to them. Both types of survey can supply you with invaluable information about communication failures, but be warned: you may not like a lot of what you discover.

Further ways of checking your communication systems are through consultative committees (see Chapter 3) and through training courses; in the latter instance, you can have all the relevant people gathered together so that you can simply ask them questions to find out how communication is working.

Finally, you can instigate an investigation of your communication procedures. Set a junior executive — say, a management trainee — the specific task of examining communication within your organisation, department, branch or whatever. The investigator should ask senior management for two or three examples of recent decisions which affect employees, and then track the communication of those decisions down through every level to the front line. Who did the manager talk to? When? How? How did the next level hear about the decision? When? How? Obviously it is important for the investigator to note if and why the news of a decision has got lost somewhere along the line, but it is equally important for him or her to find out if the *reasons* for the decision have become garbled or lost. Unknown to you, the front line may be resenting a decision of yours which, if only they knew the reasons for it, they would positively welcome.

In the remaining chapters of this book we shall look in rather more detail at the various means whereby you can communicate both upward and downward. However, all the techniques in the world are useless unless you accept the basic message: it is your duty, as a leader, to communicate, and you must do everything in your power to ensure that your communication is effective. Otherwise the efficiency of your organisation will suffer and you will be — to put it bluntly — a pretty second-rate leader.

2 TEAM BRIEFING

Team briefing is a system of communication operated by line management. Its objectives are to make sure that *all* employees know and understand what they and others in the organisation are doing, and why. It is a management information system based on leaders and their teams getting together in groups for half an hour or so on a regular basis to talk about things that are relevant to their work.

Of course, this is not some startling new piece of management theory: the Roman army used team briefing very successfully! Over the past few decades, many industrial concerns have introduced the idea of briefing groups, but all too often these have taken the form of a 'cascade' system, whereby information is merely passed from top to bottom of a company; this is all right for the first few months, when there is quite a lot of 'new' information, but once the novelty has worn off the employees become bored and senior management is left doing a lot of time-wasting floundering around trying to find something 'new' and exciting to say. The organisations that have made briefing a successful tool are those which have introduced a vital element: local information.

The most important ingredient of team briefing is, as the name implies, the team. Briefing your team is part of your leadership job: a team-briefing system merely formalises something that you do anyway if you are a good manager or supervisor. And team briefing is not a panacea: it will not improve your communication overnight. It is only one of many means of communicating information; it does not replace existing methods, but complements them. However, if your organisation does not brief information regularly through work-group leaders to their teams, then you are failing to make the first step towards good management communication.

What are the benefits of team briefing?

It is also important to remember that team briefing is not just a way of keeping everyone happy. As a by-product, it does indeed enrich your employees' working lives, but more importantly it increases your organisation's efficiency. It does so in several different ways.

First, it reinforces management all the way down the line. The very act of getting the team together means that the manager is *seen to be the leader.* This is particularly important in the lower echelons of management, where often supervisors, having failed to receive any reminder of the fact that they have responsibilities, quite naturally regard the fact that they have a larger pay packet than their fellows as simply recognition of their experience, expertise, or both. They *forget* that they are a part of management — and there is no reason why they should remember, unless you make it happen through team briefing. A graphic example was supplied a few years ago in a West Country company when a shop-floor supervisor showed reluctance to the idea of briefing her subordinates. When asked why she did not want to, she said that it was not part of her job: briefing was *management's* job. When asked what she thought differentiated her from the other women on the line, her stark response was: 'More money.' It was only after she herself had received team briefing that she realised that she, too, had responsibility to help her own team get the best results. She soon recognised that it was the responsibility that differentiated her from the others, not just 'more money'.

Second, team briefing increases people's commitment to the task in which their team is involved as well as to the objectives of the organisation as a whole. People need to be told how they are doing as a team, and whether or not they are achieving their targets. Clearly, it is extremely hard to be committed to something when you do not actually know what that something *is!* Talking to people regularly about how the team is doing and how various specific problems are being overcome gives people an objective. Of course, briefing will not make a boring job interesting, but it will give the work a purpose and the person doing it some form of direction. Explaining *why* something needs to be done is as important as explaining how to do it. Even if a person does not agree with the reasons they are being asked to do something, they will do it if they understand the underlying rationale. Other important aspects of improved commitment are:

- less absenteeism
- less wastage
- greater productivity
- improved awareness of safety and good housekeeping
- cost savings

In this last respect, many organisations have discovered that by merely *telling* employees the size of the quarterly telephone bill, and how to reduce it (for example, by phoning in the afternoons rather than the mornings), colossal savings can be made.

A third advantage of team briefing is that it helps reduce misunderstandings. In many organisations, the left hand doesn't seem to know what the right hand is doing. Misunderstandings can be costly, time-consuming, and embarrassing. If you are a good leader you will not mind being embarrassed from time to time — it's fun for all concerned — but you will mind about the wastage of time and money. In one large company the Finance Director unilaterally changed the procedure for signing invoices, and communicated the fact only through memos to the management team. For days thereafter, people lower down the ladder wasted vast amounts of time trying to find out what the new system was — and often even more time was wasted because someone 'thought' they knew the new system but thought wrong. In terms of man-hours, the cost was huge; further, the Finance Director was no longer regarded as an effective leader, which again reduced the company's efficiency. A little while spent on team briefing could have avoided all this.

Advantage number four is that team briefing helps people accept change. Most of us do not like change: we are insecure when faced with something we are not used to. Workforces have been known to strike over matters as trivial as moving offices — even when the new offices were more desirable — simply because of a lack of down-the-line communication. Yet in other companies people have accepted redundancies without protest purely because they have been kept informed as to why those redundancies are necessary.

Fifth, team briefing helps control the grapevine. If you think your organisation has no grapevine, that is probably because it has a whole vineyard! Team briefing will not get rid of the grapevine — or vineyard — but it will certainly help control it. Of course, people will always listen to the grapevine first — the news is always that much more scandalous — but if there is a briefing system, they will wait to listen to the 'official' version from their manager before coming to any conclusion. Moreover, managers will be better informed than they would have been had they had no other way of knowing what employees thought except through hearing things on the grapevine 'on the way up'.

In relation to this, team briefing certainly does improve the communication of information upwards. Some senior managers find it difficult to understand why people do not seem to have good ideas or even views about what is going on. Why does the consultative committee always discuss the chips in the canteen or — even worse — the dreaded coffee machine? Why has no one put anything other than obscene remarks in the suggestions box? Lack of information and understanding is often at the heart of all this. Team-briefing meetings should not be used for consultation or problem solving — mixing two objectives merely confuses the issue — but feedback as a result of these meetings is a common side benefit and, if harnessed, can vitalise or revitalise the upward communication system.

How to implement team briefing: five cardinal principles

Team briefing is a simple concept — but the simplest things are often, paradoxically, the most difficult to attain. Over the years, organisations that have introduced team briefing have found that an initial investment of time and money will bring lasting benefits. Some organisations, by contrast, have attempted to initiate briefing systems simply by announcing to all concerned that in future there will be monthly meetings, and expecting that things will just 'happen'.

If you want to implement team briefing successfully, there are a number of things you must do.

First, it is essential that you, yourself, are thoroughly committed to the idea and are prepared to be involved in its implementation; it helps if the senior management team are committed as well. Ideally, the decision to institute team briefing in your organisation should be taken at board level, or at least among senior management. Likewise, union representatives need to be fully informed of any team-briefing scheme, and should be able to ask questions about it. In fact, the inauguration of a team-briefing scheme should have little or no impact on union concerns, but courtesy in this context will forestall any possible adverse reactions to what might in some way be perceived as a 'threat'. The commitment of the union representatives will help assure the commitment of the rest of the workforce — as indeed will the full-blooded commitment of all the managers and supervisors who are going to be involved in briefing teams. You should try to make sure that, before team briefing starts, a course is held to train all the briefers.

For the scheme to be successful, you need to appoint some individual as a coordinator. This person should be carefully selected: he or she must have enough time to organise the project properly, but should also be senior enough to have the necessary authority. He or she should fully comprehend the structure of the organisation, and all the ladders of accountability within it. The managing director is usually a poor choice as coordinator — he or she rarely has the requisite time — and so the best bet is usually the personnel manager, the communication manager if there is one, or, occasionally, the factory manager.

Outside advice and help give a tremendous advantage. While the coordinator supplies the inside knowledge and drive, the outsider brings credibility and the experience of other organisations' systems. However, you should not think that the use of an outsider negates the need for an internal coordinator — far from it. The coordinator's role is vital, both in setting up the system and, once it is functioning, in maintaining it.

Team briefing will not just 'happen' because the managing director says it should. There needs to be a structure and drill that can be monitored. The structure makes sure that everybody knows who briefs whom and in which teams, and the drill lays down when it should happen and how often. The details of the structure and drill for each organisation will differ, but there are five fundamental principles that have to be observed. Successful team briefing must be

- face-to-face
- in teams
- given by the team leader
- regular
- relevant

We've already seen in Chapter 1 why face-to-face communication is important, but why should *teams,* preferably of between four and fifteen people, be such an important factor in briefing? Well, even though, if you are a good manager, you regularly talk to individuals about the things that affect them, team briefing gives you the opportunity to talk over with your team the matters that affect all of them. It is a lot quicker than speaking to everybody individually, and it makes sure that you do not accidentally miss someone out (it is far too easy to do this when walking the job, so that you can omit speaking with some individuals for months on end — bad practice!). All the people in the team know that you have given them exactly the same information: if you informed them all individually, some would feel that they had been told a different story than others — and probably would have been, since it is almost impossible to convey exactly the same message to a dozen people individually. Also, as we saw on page 6, the potential for understanding is far greater when you are dealing with a group than when you are dealing with individuals — simply because the answer to one person's question may assist or correct the understanding of another person. Finally, the fact that the team is meeting together is a tremendous motivator: all the team members gain the impression that they are working together towards a common goal.

Someone has to be the leader in team briefing, and he or she must be accountable for the performance of the team being briefed. Sometimes, this may mean that the team-briefing hierarchy is different from the organisation's customary one: it may well be, in some circumstances, that the departmental boss is not the ideal person to brief the team. You have to be careful about whom you specify to be the briefer — especially when people report to more than one manager. Wherever possible, opt for a task-oriented, rather than a function-oriented team, and choose your briefer accordingly. Also, give some thought to the size of the team: if there are less than four or more than fifteen people involved, the whole exercise is likely to be pointless. It is easy enough to decide the sizes of the teams being briefed by opting for the correct management level: if the teams are too small, go for someone in the next echelon upward, so that he or she can brief a group of ten or twelve; likewise, if the teams are too large, go for someone in the next echelon downward as the briefer.

Regularity is important. Most organisations which have incorporated team briefing brief once a month, because this period is related to the board or senior-management meetings, which themselves relate to the organisation's accounting periods. Whatever the frequency, the regularity should not vary: regularity breeds credibility, and briefing should never come to be regarded as an *ad hoc* activity. The frequency is important, too: less than once a month and you are wasting your time.

The final cardinal principle of good team briefing is relevance. The key to this is good local information: at least 70 per cent of the brief should consist of local information, with no more than 30 per cent being handed down from above. It is not enough just to ask people to add local information to the brief supplied by senior management, because in practice people usually get bored of doing this, so that after the first few sessions all you are doing is passing on senior management's brief verbatim. What you require is a drill to ensure that there is a high level of local input.

An engineering company in Glasgow has come up with a simple drill that solved the problem. They ask their supervisors to prepare their own briefing notes prior to their meetings with their managers. A couple of days before the main procedures start, the supervisors write down the points on which they want to brief their teams. They talk these points through with their managers, or show them their written brief, and the managers add in any points coming either from themselves or from senior management. In other words, the whole emphasis is turned around: the briefing consists of the supervisor's points with those of management added, rather than of management's points with the supervisor's added. Not only is the briefing more effective because it contains a lot of local information, the points made by senior management are put over with more enthusiasm and commitment by the supervisor.

The easiest way to ensure that this sort of system works is to request that supervisors bring along to their briefing meetings the points that they will wish to make when briefing their own team. This allows you to check that the local points have in fact been prepared; it gives you valuable feedback concerning what the local issues are at the next level down; and, because each supervisor hears what the others have to say, there is a useful cross-fertilisation of ideas.

This checking of local briefing points is crucial. You may find it a bit of an uphill struggle at first, because managers and supervisors always 'have something better to do', but it is worth persevering. Apart from anything else, it means that, at least once a month, supervisors sit down to consider how the job is going and how it might be done better — in effect, you are getting them to think like the managers they may one day become, and that just has to be good for the organisation.

Implementation: further considerations

Aside from the five cardinal principles, there are a few other considerations which ought to be in your mind when you are implementing a team-briefing system.

First, there should not be too many levels of briefing — otherwise the story being recounted on the shop floor will be a hideously garbled version of what you want to put across. Ideally, there should be no more than four levels. If your organisation is a very large one (over 10,000 people), so that this is impossible without briefing being given to teams of more than fifteen people, it is worth trying to see if the whole exercise cannot be subdivided — by task or by site, for example.

Timing is another important issue. Team briefings should take place at a set time, and it may be worth your while settling this as much as a year ahead. All the briefings need to take place within a period of 48 hours, to make sure that the grapevine does not pass on the news before the briefings do. It is also a good idea if all the people at a particular level are briefed simultaneously, and so you have to think hard about exactly when you can cease all work at that level for half an hour or so. If this is not possible, perhaps because the work is continuous-process work, see if you can keep things ticking over with a skeleton crew, who can be briefed immediately after their comrades. Clearly, simultaneity is impossible if people are working in shifts; nevertheless, you should try to ensure that the meetings take place as close as possible to each other.

Although, as always, paperwork should be kept to a minimum, a number of documents can be useful. You should have a policy document, setting out for all to see your approach to team briefing and how it will work in practice; this document will obviously have to be revised from time to time, as people leave or the organisation is restructured, but the effort is worth it because this is the 'Bible' of your team-briefing system. Briefing forms can be important, too: they should provide the briefer with an accurate version of the points management wishes to make, as well as plenty of space so that he or she can itemise the local points and keep a record of issues arising from questions. Allied to this, briefers should have feedback forms so that, if they are unable to answer a question on the spot, they can note it on the form, pass it up the ladder, and be assured that within at most 48 hours they will receive a reply that they can pass on to their subordinates.

Finally, all briefers need to be trained for the task. This will almost certainly require the use of courses. The three objectives of these courses should be to ensure commitment to the team-briefing system, to communicate understanding of how the system operates and why, and to help briefers develop the necessary skills for effective preparation and presentation of a brief. As soon as possible after the courses are completed, team briefing should begin — it is a bad idea to leave it too long, as otherwise some of the benefits of the courses will be lost through people forgetting what they have learned or just becoming bored with the idea. Some companies prefer to start with a dry run, down to supervisor level only, in order to test the system out, and certainly this can help you isolate and iron out problems before you go the whole hog.

What to talk about

As we have seen, it is vital that the information being briefed is relevant — that is, local — to the people whom you are briefing. But there are a few other important considerations.

You must get straight in your head the correct balance between what the team *needs* to be told and what it would *like* to be told. Team briefing is a way of communicating information that management *needs people to know*. Under no circumstances should it be allowed to degenerate into nothing more than a welcome break from work, with a few jokes and some banal facts selected only in order to keep the team members riveted to their seats. Some briefers become quite neurotic trying to find ways of making team briefings interesting — but it is not necessary, and it may quite probably be counterproductive.

Another thing to remember is that this is a briefing, not a discussion. Senior management should have provided an initial typed brief, to which points have been added by people progressively further down the ladder; to these you will have added your own specific points. If you have, in all, ten points (which is probably too many) to get over to the team in thirty minutes, this means that to each point you can devote, on average, three minutes. So stick to those points, and do not be distracted into other areas. Explain the points fully and, obviously, answer questions about them, but never make the mistake of allowing the meeting to become a general chat. When people ask you irrelevant questions — and they certainly will — arrange to answer them afterwards. If you become involved in a contentious issue, cut the discussion short, explain that there is a time constraint, and agree to come back to it another time, when you will be absolutely certain of the facts and the reasons behind them.

On the subject of questions, it is a good idea to ask a few yourself, just to make sure that the team is attending to and understanding what you are trying to convey. Remember, the most interested-looking face can often belong to the person who is in fact thinking about what they are going to do after work that day.

In the ideal briefing, there should be four main subject areas:

- progress
- policy
- people
- points for action

All four should be raised during the meeting, although of course it is not necessary to be rigid about the presentation: if news about promotions comes in the middle of your spiel about points for action, for example, it does not actually matter much, just so long as all the necessary information is conveyed.

For effective briefing, it is virtually essential that you convey as much information as possible by the use of examples, rather than by discussion of abstract theory. Examples create a much more vivid impression in people's minds, and they are usually much more interesting — they may even be funny (although, remember, you are there to inform people, not to amuse them). Saying 'I think our safety standards have slipped and we must all make an effort to pull our socks up because safety is very important' is a far less effective way of communicating your message than 'Last week George nearly broke his leg because he fell over a box which some clown had left lying in a gangway — so let's keep the gangways clear or someone is going to break their neck'.

Remember to present good news; in fact, it is worth noting down good news as it happens, because otherwise you are likely to forget it by the time of the briefing session. It is always much easier to remember bad news and, while no one likes it, this too has to be presented at the meeting. Whatever you do, though, do not let this turn the meeting into a sort of disciplinary session; in contrast, try to use a positive approach to the bad news: say why it has come about and what the organisation is doing to rectify things — and what the team itself can do to help. And take a positive attitude towards the bad news: you will turn people off if you say, 'We didn't meet our targets last month — in fact, we did really badly,' but you can get a real benefit from the bad news if you rephrase this as: 'We failed to meet our targets last month, but there's no reason why we can't pick up some of the loss next month and break even by the end of the year if we ...'

Of course, if you have been communicating effectively on a day-to-day basis, there will not be too much actual 'news' for you to present at the meeting. Do not worry about this. Day-to-day communication tends to be a somewhat haphazard affair. At a team briefing you can put together all the disparate pieces of news that have amassed during the month and present your team with a coherent overall picture. It is rather like the difference between looking at the individual frames of a movie, not necessarily in the right order, and watching the movie itself. Looking at each frame gives you a lot of detail, but watching the movie tells you what that detail means. Also, at the briefing session, you can give a quick preview of 'next month's movie', which will make the information given day-to-day — the 'frames' — that much more relevant, because it will be understood in context.

Another point on the 'news' front is that team briefing allows you to give the Official Version. People will probably already have heard just about all your news on the grapevine, and there is a high chance, as we have seen, that the information will have become distorted. This is your chance to present the truth of the matter — or, at least, the 'truth' management would like to convey, which might be subtly different. For example, in one company everybody 'knew' that a director had been fired because it had emerged that he was a homosexual. In fact, despite the protestations of the rest of the board, he had resigned because he was embarrassed that they knew about his homosexuality. It was briefed to the staff simply that he had resigned 'for personal reasons', and soon the matter of his homosexuality was widely regarded as nothing more than a rumour. Of course, he was foolish to regard his homosexuality as a 'guilty secret', but this very slight managerial distortion of the truth did not really mislead the staff, and meant that the ex-director was a lot happier whenever he met the company's employees in the street.

So, even if you have no really new information to convey, do not consider that your presentation of information is a waste of time. Far from it: the briefing session allows you to correct people's false impressions, to remind people of things they may have forgotten, to highlight the more important events of the last month, and to present all the information in the way that you — and your superiors — want it to be presented.

What if people object?

Team briefing is based on common sense and good management practice, but you are likely to hear a number of voices raised in objection to the idea of instituting it. Let us look at a few examples of the kinds of objections you are likely to encounter.

'We all do this already'

This objection is normally voiced by a member of senior management, and in a limited way it is true. Senior managers do indeed communicate regularly with each other, and frequently have monthly meetings with their immediate subordinates. However, it is only rarely that this is carried through right down to the front line. Unless there is a system which can be monitored, and in which the information is passed on by someone who can be held accountable for doing so, communication is unlikely to cross the 'supervisor barrier'. One of the good things about team briefing is that managers *know* that people are being told.

Also, it is highly unlikely that, in any given organisation, *all* the managers and supervisors are communicating effectively to their subordinates. There are always a few who are perennially too busy to get around to it, or who have the petty-mindedness to think that knowledge is power, or who simply do not enjoy communicating and so do it as rarely as possible, or who do their best but are just rank *bad* at communicating. A system ensures that *everyone* briefs, all the way down the line — not just the people who would brief their subordinates anyway. Of course, if it is really true that 'we all do this already', then your organisation is engaged in team briefing without realising it; but, unless a conscious decision has been made to institute a system, this is pretty improbable.

'They already know everything'

This is a common cry of finance directors or accounts managers, who feel that all their people know everything they need to know purely because it is all contained in the work passing across their desks. The only answer to this objection is: 'No, they don't.' It is perfectly true that all the pertinent information about a company may be contained in the work a person is doing, but it is in a jumbled, fragmented form — rather like a jigsaw puzzle. Few of our subordinates have the time or inclination to put all the pieces of the puzzle together, and indeed it is a waste of the organisation's efficiency should they have to do so. Someone needs to put the puzzle together and then show the picture to everyone else.

'It will cost too much/take too much time'

Installing team briefing does cost money and it does take time. It is, however, an investment in your organisation's future success: once the system has been set up, it will last forever, so that after the first few months the only real expenditure is that of time, meaning that, on average, it costs about 0.3 per cent of productive time! Team briefing needs to have only the tiniest degree of effectiveness in order to make this up.

However, when inaugurating the system, it is important not to stint in terms of either time or money. If the system fails because of management's lack of commitment, the workforce will regard it as having been nothing more than yet another management 'flavour of the month'. The loss of management credibility will be damaging, but more important will be the fact that it will be years before you can have another bite of the cherry — people will, quite rationally, respond that 'we tried team briefing once and it didn't work, so why should we try it again?'

'Our supervisors/foremen couldn't brief'

Oh yes they could.

Most supervisors and foremen can brief adequately after just a little training to boost their confidence and give them a few tips. Some people will always be better than others at briefing their teams, and a few will never be able to manage it. But bear in mind that you are not trying to train them to be slick after-dinner speakers: all you are aiming for is that they be good enough. It is a great mistake to prejudge someone's ability or inability to brief: you will find that some of the most unexpected people are very good at it, and also that a great many supervisors become very much better at their jobs overall when they are given the opportunity to brief their people. In many cases, you can do your shyer subordinates a real favour by *forcing* them to brief: often it can transform their personalities, turn them into really effective leaders, and vastly enrich their lives.

'The unions won't let us'

Oh yes they will.

Team briefing is a management system for communicating management information and explaining the management message. In no way does it undercut the role of the unions, or of the union representatives: their job is to convey employees' concerns to management, and they are usually only too glad to be relieved of the unfair burden of explaining management's concerns to the employees. And, the better informed the workforce, the easier the task of the union representative, because he or she goes to management with all the pertinent facts at his or her fingertips.

On occasion, you may find that union representatives regard the communication of information as their prerogative. This is almost always because, in the past, management has been failing to do its job properly. In such a situation, change will not come about overnight: you have to persuade the representatives to accept team briefing by stressing the benefits it has for them, for the employees, and for the well-being of the organisation as a whole — all of which will take time. However, it is worth the effort. You will usually find that the unions' regional organisers will be only too eager to help you.

'It's too formal for our informal management style'

This may indeed be true in a small company, but if a company has more than about fifty employees it may prove difficult to retain informality while maintaining efficiency. In fact, a system of team briefing is a great help here, because the briefers can be as informal as they like, yet the very fact that the system has a structure ensures that important information is passed on to everybody. Likewise, people can communicate as informally as they wish on a day-to-day basis, yet know they can rely on the monthly team-briefing sessions to ensure that all the information has indeed been correctly conveyed. 'Structured informality' would seem to be a safer bet for company stability than 'informal structuring'. So by all means preserve your informality — it is often the sign of a happy company — but bear in mind that team briefing can help you preserve it.

'People will just use the system to moan'

Meetings can easily turn into moaning sessions, but only if the briefer allows them to. It needs to be quite clear, when you inaugurate the system, that the objective of the briefing sessions is to pass on information and to answer questions about that information. (This is one of the reasons why it is so important to train the briefers properly.) If people try to air grievances they should be reminded quite firmly of the grievance procedure, or directed to the relevant union or staff representative. Team briefing sessions are not consultation, nor negotiation, nor a way of problem solving: they are simply information sessions in which there is the opportunity to ask questions.

In short, people will use the briefing sessions as opportunities for a good moan only if they are allowed to. It is very easy to make sure they are not allowed to.

'After the first few briefs we'll run out of information'

If team briefing is being operated properly, it is virtually impossible to run out of information: more commonly, the problem is to cut down the information so that it can all be fitted into half an hour!

If the system is allowed to rely heavily on information from on high, then you may run into difficulties, but there is always relevant information to talk about at local level. This means that each briefer has to be trained to write his or her own brief, rather than being used by management merely as a 'postbox' to pass on information.

The general response to all of these objections, then, is that, yes, they may be valid if team briefing is ineptly organised and executed. If you put just a little bit more effort into setting up and maintaining the system, then all of the objections are nullified.

Team briefing lays the foundation for the development of employees' involvement at work. If management is unaware of this, there will almost inevitably soon be a general atmosphere of despondency in the organisation, because management seems to be interested in telling, not in listening. Team briefing cannot and should not be used as a method of upward as well as downward communication, but it does provide an important starting point from which the channels of upward communication can be developed — perhaps through separate meetings.

So, if you wish to be effective communicator, team briefing is a vital component of your armoury.

Checklist

How do I prepare?
- put items in my briefing folder during the month
- go to my briefing with my own local brief already written
- add the relevant matters from my team leader's brief to my own local brief
- ask questions to ensure I understand, and cover the points my team needs to know about

How do I go about briefing?
- plan what I want to say and keep it simple
- use examples, and make the message relevant to my team
- keep to the subject
- encourage questions on the information I brief
- remember I am briefing the management view
- record questions I cannot answer and then get the answer back to the questioner

- brief absentees immediately when they return to work

What subjects should I brief?

- progress — the regular yardsticks of how my team is doing against target, quality standard, and so on (highlighting good performances)
- policy — those procedures, policies or decisions that affect my team which need to be explained or reemphasised
- people — anything that affects my team
- points for action — what are the priorities for the months, what can we improve on, and do any procedures or drills need to be explained?

3 CONSULTATION

Consultation is the process whereby, on a regular basis, management genuinely seeks the views, ideas and feelings of employees before a decision is taken. The International Labour Organization defines consultation as being 'where one party genuinely seeks the views of another party before either party takes a decision'. If you are to be an effective communicator, then consultation is one of your most important tools.

Consultation can

- improve the quality of decisions, because you are using the collected knowledge and ingenuity of those who are most affected by your decisions
- stimulate better cooperation between managers and employees, because people will accept even those decisions they do not like if their views have been taken into account (and assuming they have been told why the decision has been taken)
- serve as a valuable preliminary to negotiation: when representatives have been involved in the discussion of 'how?' they will certainly be better informed and probably more realistic when it becomes a matter of 'how much?'
- increase the efficiency of the entire organisation by involving employees in achieving a better product or providing a better service
- help industrial relations, through allowing managers and employees the opportunity to understand each other's views and objectives

There are many ways in which upward communication can be improved: walking the job (see page 13) is the obvious one. You can talk with people, chat with them on social occasions, set up special working parties, work alongside your subordinates and, above all, listen to them. But in larger organisations — perhaps even those with as few as a hundred employees — this is not enough. You can of course get some of the facts of a situation by hearing or receiving views as reported upwards through the various levels of the leadership chain, but what you will be getting is a watered-down and possibly distorted version of the truth: it is no substitute for what you will hear directly from the person who is actually doing the job.

Consultation systems are not new. They were installed decades ago by such forward-looking companies as Colman's (1909), Kalamazoo (1913), the forerunners of ICI Mond (1920), and United Steel (1928). After World War I, Whitley Councils were introduced to the Government Service. Many companies have since followed suit, particularly as a result of the boost of 'joint production committees' during World War II and of the growth of the trade-union movement during the 1940s and 1950s.

Nowadays, few British companies with more than 250 employees do not have some mechanism for consultation. However, often this has not developed beyond the cumbersome old-style systems which have proved so frustrating both to managers and to representatives. Consequently, in many companies the whole notion has lost its credibility, because managers have allowed consultation to fall by the wayside during times of crisis, and have become disillusioned by the amount of trivia discussed by consultative committees or quality circles (see Chapter 4).

Whatever the system used, the aim is to seek the ideas and views of the people who actually create the goods and services in the factory or office, and you should never lose sight of this. You have to accept, as a decision-maker, that you alone do not possess a monopoly of all the bright ideas, and that your decision is likely to be half-baked unless you have a vivid first-hand impression of your employees' views. You must realise that it is vital to have a channel of communication whereby you can hear the opinions of those who have to put your decisions into practice.

What consultation is not

Consultation is neither a means of communicating management information downward nor an excuse to 'address the troops'. If management allows it to become so, then representatives are put in the invidious position of being the sole communicators of management's messages. Management should use team briefing (see Chapter 2) if they have information they want to impart. The whole point of consultation is that it provides for communication upward, not downward.

Like team briefing, consultation should be something more than a means of keeping the employees happy. While obviously the employees like to be consulted and know that their ideas are being taken into account, the main aim of consultation is to improve the organisation's performance through discovering the frequently valuable information possessed by those in the front line.

Consultation meetings are not negotiation meetings. Negotiation is a quite separate process, and the two should never be confused. Allowing them to become so works to the detriment of both managers and workforce.

As with team-briefing sessions, consultation meetings should never be allowed to degenerate into epics of group moaning, or extended discussions of the state of the toilets. There are other avenues along which these items (which are not always as trivial as they seem) can be pursued — unless they are directly relevant to the organisation's efficiency. For example, one large company suffered a great deal of industrial unrest until, during consultation, an employee pointed out to management that people's tempers were less likely to be volatile if it were not the company rule that, should an employee spend more than five minutes in the lavatory, the foreman would be sent to shout through the door to tell the person to get a move on! Management realized the folly of the practice, stopped it, restored the dignity of their employees, and were delighted when there was a significant drop in the number of wildcat strikes.

Such examples are the exception, however: generally it is essential, if consultation is to be effective, that the discussion should be steered clear of 'negative' topics. The aim of consultation is to put into effect the belief that employees, just as much as management, have rights — and responsibilities — to help do their part in ensuring the smooth and productive running of the organisation, so that everybody can benefit.

Basic principles of consultation

Any system of consultation will rapidly lose its credibility — will be seen to be nothing more than cosmetic — unless the actual consultation takes place before decisions are made, and is *seen* to be so. You must 'be sincere in seeking the views of your employees about changes that will affect them *before* you take your final decision. Even after the decision has been made, it can be valuable to consult how best to put it into practice.

Regularity is another important point: if consultation happens only from time to time, seemingly at your whim, your employees will lose all faith in it — and quite right too. The frequency of meetings has to be agreed, established, and adhered to. Even in hard times, it is vital to continue the pattern if you are going to achieve your subordinates' cooperation and make sound decisions which will then be effectively communicated throughout the organisation.

Consultation should be initiated by management. It is *your* task to take the initiative, to introduce change, and to gain commitment throughout the organisation. You must demonstrate your conviction that consultation is an integral part of your decision-making process, and therefore you should take the lead in proposing items for consultative discussion. This is not to say that employees should not be allowed to suggest items for discussion — far from it! — but, particularly in the early stages of a consultative system, the larger part of the time should be spent on items put forward by management.

However, you should try to ensure that union representatives, wherever possible, play a large part in consultation: not only may they make a valuable contribution, it will help you when you are negotiating with those same representatives if they understand exactly what is going on, and why — especially if their contribution has been a significant part of the 'why'. Also, of course, it is a matter of common courtesy to include the unions in your consultations; if you do not, you can hardly blame their representatives if they develop a feeling of 'Them' and 'Us'.

Finally, as with team briefing, relevance is something to consider. Experience has shown that, the more 'local' the items being discussed, the more valuable will be the outcome.

Structuring consultation

Obviously, different companies will have different ways in which consultation can best be established. Their approaches will differ according to the type of business, size, dispersal, relations with unions, management style, and the percentage of decisions that lend themselves to consultation at different levels. However, we can establish a few general trends.

The various levels of an organisation at which consultation proves most efficacious are as follows:

- Work-group level. Here, front-line managers call together their team to examine improvements that could be made in their own area.
- Site, division or unit level (perhaps 250 employees). Senior managers meet up with employees' representatives to look at wider issues relevant to the unit as a whole. At this level unit-wide issues should be brought up, managers should consult the representatives as a *de rigueur* part of their decision-making process, representatives should bring unit-wide concerns to the forefront, and useful points from the work-group level should be fully debated.
- Group level. This applies to larger companies. At the most senior levels there will be fewer points to discuss that are common to all concerned, but nevertheless this level is important because it endorses the entire consultation structure throughout the organisation, and gives it maximum credibility. These meetings must monitor consultation throughout the group and ensure that senior managers meet with senior employee representatives on common ground.

This is a useful general structure, but many companies have found it far more effective and practical to go one step further and involve as many employees as possible in decisions which affect them and in looking at the day-to-day problems they encounter.

At work-group level you have to accept the fact that some employees simply will not be interested, or will be interested only in a specific (and possibly trivial) problem — even though others will be enthusiastic about the whole concept. You can put the enthusiasm of these latter to good use by setting up a quality circle. We shall discuss this topic in more detail in the next chapter, but it's worth looking briefly at it here.

Quality circles are small groups of volunteers who meet regularly with their immediate boss in an attempt to identify and solve their own work-related problems. If the authority of putting their suggestions into practice lies with the boss, then they go right ahead; if others are involved in the authorisation process, the group presents its findings to a group of managers. The final decision to implement a proposed change always rests with management but, clearly, if the enthusiasm to maintain a quality circle is to be maintained, management's response must be both speedy and explicit.

There are significant potential benefits in this type of local-level consultation. Because everyone present shares the task in common, they can investigate it in close-up and often come out with blinding realisations of the obvious. The outcome is not just a more efficient organisation: you also have employees who are less frustrated because they themselves have been permitted to make a practical contribution to making their own area more successful. In addition, the credibility of front-line managers is vastly increased when it is seen that it really is worthwhile to take one's opinions to them.

One danger with quality circles is that they can become elitist and run out of ideas if they do not have the back-up of good communication with the rest of the team. If a front-line manager wants to consult employees before making a decision, it is important that he or she should speak to the *whole* team, not just to the enthusiasts in the quality circle. So, at the end of a monthly briefing, as a separate item, or as part of a departmental meeting, front-line managers should ensure that everyone is informed about what is going on and be receptive to ideas from people outside the quality circle.

Quality circles can, of course, look at issues outside their own province, but unless this local-level consultation is backed up by consultation at a more senior level and across the departments, employees will in the long term become frustrated because their discussions of wider issues will be seen as being useless or, worse, being ignored or rejected by management.

Consultation at unit level is rather different. Those attending a unit consultative committee may not necessarily be specialists on every aspect of the business or have an intimate and detailed knowledge of every problem. Many companies therefore encourage consultative committees to set up specialist project groups of volunteers from all sides and levels of the organisation who have a particular interest in and/or knowledge of a specific problem. These subgroups, which report back to the consultative committee, can achieve significant improvements in company systems, policies, coordination, and so forth. A graphic example was provided in 1981-83 when it was stated that Austin Rover, through the implementation of the cost-cutting ideas of 'think tanks' drawn from employees from the shop floor upwards, had saved no less than twenty million pounds! It is hardly surprising that more and more employers are realising that the involvement of people at work is not just a more civilised way of going about things but also a sensible way of doing business.

Consultative committees will rarely attempt to resolve problems: their real function is to identify the problem and then establish a project group of volunteers to find possible solutions and report back their findings. Where the committee is at work-group level, such project groups should institute their activities weekly or fortnightly, and their results should be discussed at the end of every monthly team meeting. Project groups at unit level should swing into action as soon as any problem is identified; their results should be reported every two months, if not more often. All of these results should be collated and discussed at group level no less frequently than twice a year — otherwise the effort is wasted, because the problem has either solved itself (usually to the organisation's detriment) or has become so endemic within the organisation that it will be virtually impossible to eradicate it. It is rather like having bindweed in your garden: strike early and fast, using everything in your armoury, or you will be stuck with the stuff forever.

The project-group structure has several great strengths. For example, although it seems to involve a great many meetings, these are all brief, and they are devoted to *solving* rather than merely discussing problems. In the longer term, greater benefits result — and certainly less time is wasted in futile generalised meetings discussing specialised subjects. Moreover, the system can be constructed from the bottom up, by developing problem-solving consultation and involvement at the local level and then building up to the unit level. Finally, a plan can be developed to gradually install a consultation system over a period of time. In many organisations, managers have to build up their credibility as 'listeners' slowly, and give employees time to adapt to the new, cooperative atmosphere.

How to make a consultative committee work best

Having too large a committee limits individual participation and makes control difficult. By contrast, if the committee is too small you will not encounter the wide range of views that makes consultation such an effective tool of management. Experience has shown that a committee of about twelve people is the ideal.

The committee should meet regularly — once every couple of months, if not more often. If bi-monthly meetings tend to last for over two hours, it is a good idea to hold them more frequently and keep them shorter: most people get sick of a meeting after the first hour and a half, and stop making any positive contribution, in the hope that if they keep quiet the whole blasted thing will be over soon. Whatever the frequency you opt for, it is a very good idea to fix the dates for forthcoming meetings a full year in advance, and to do everything in your power to stick to the programme.

In addition to the regular meetings, it is a good idea to hold extraordinary meetings should the occasion arise — either at the request of management or if a certain number of committee members think it is necessary.

Voting and decision-taking do not — or, most certainly, should not — take place during consultation, and so there is no real need to ensure equality in numbers between management and employee representatives, except insofar as it is a bad plan to have too many management representatives, because then the employees feel outnumbered and are reluctant to come out with their ideas. The ideal seems to be about one management representative to two or three employee representatives. The management representatives should be nominated, not elected, and should comprise a cross-section of the management chain all the way down from senior management to front-line supervisors. The personnel manager may need to be at all consultation meetings, and the personnel department may have to supply a secretary — although the committee members may prefer to elect a secretary themselves.

Management nominees must understand clearly that they are part of the management team, and are not attending as representatives of their colleagues: they are representing neither other managers, who are unlikely, anyway, to use a consultative committee to raise points, nor employees, as it is impossible simultaneously to represent and manage. Continuity is important; nevertheless, in the course of each twelvemonth as many individual managers as possible should have the experience of participating in a consultative committee. Some companies, in establishing their managers' targets, insist on attendance of a consultative committee at least once a year.

The leader of the committee and all participating managers should understand that they are expected to contribute freely to the consultation meetings. When managers take the initiative they stimulate and expand discussion, so that employee representatives find it easier to join in and contribute more wholeheartedly.

In organisations where trade unions have negotiating rights, the best plan is often that shop stewards represent employees in consultation as well as in negotiation. Negotiation often involves conflict, and so it is good for both managers and shop stewards if they can have the opportunity of meeting each other in the far more constructive ambience of the consultative committee.

Ideally, each employee representative on the committee should represent about 30 constituents, and certainly no more than about 60 — because, the greater the number of constituents, the more difficult it is adequately to canvass and digest their opinions. This can cause problems of equality between the unions, because one shop steward may represent a handful of skilled workers and another 90 per cent of the workforce. If you can, try to get the unions to agree among themselves about a fairer distribution of representatives: perhaps one representative could act for the members of several different unions, or one union could have several representatives. This problem of the size of a representative's constituency needs some careful thinking on your part. An overriding consideration is that, as far as possible, people who work for the same manager or who do the same sort of work should be grouped together, because of their common interests and expertise.

The leader of the consultative committee should normally be the senior manager of the unit. This is important, because it emphasises the fact that management is taking the committee seriously, and because senior managers are the people who can gain most from receiving, first-hand, the views of the committee's members. Even if, for one reason or another, someone else is installed as the committee's leader, the senior manager should be present at the meetings — or, *in extremis,* should appoint

40

someone to report back in detail. This should be very much a last resort, though: it is inefficient and time-wasting, and it creates the risk that points will be distorted or forgotten.

It is important that the meeting should have a proper agenda, prepared and circulated at least five days beforehand. Both management and employees should initiate items for the agenda — and it is one of your responsibilities to ensure that employees are encouraged to contribute items. Every item on the agenda should be clearly stated and supported by relevant information, explanatory notes, and so on; otherwise it is impossible for managers and representatives to prepare their thoughts and canvass the views of their colleagues. It can be helpful if employee representatives have a preliminary meeting so that they are fully *au fait* with all the points that are going to be discussed; however, there is a danger that they will come to a common consensus on various issues, and try to use the consultative committee as a forum for negotiation.

It is vital that the results of committee meetings are reported back to employees as soon as possible. Minutes — which should be brief (one page is best) — should be distributed within 24 hours and displayed on the notice-board, and the organisation's house journal should carry a lively account of the discussions. Obviously, the results of the meeting should be a part of team-briefing sessions, and it may be worth setting up a mass meeting. An annual report of the workings of the consultative committees should be issued, perhaps in video form. Remember that employees' interest is encouraged if you publicise the existence of the consultative committees and build up their reputation as an opportunity for the employees' voices to be heard.

Avoiding frustration

The main cause of frustration in any consultation exercise is trivia. One survey of the minutes of consultative meetings in a retail chain showed that, on average, at every meeting three separate items were discussed regarding the canteen. Of course, the canteen is an important matter and any problems concerning it should be looked at, but it is not so important that it should dominate the agenda.

In some cases, the system itself and lack of management planning are responsible for the fact that the agendas have so few 'real' items on them. However, the real way of reducing the amount of 'clutter' seems to be a question of changing the outlook of everyone concerned — managers, representatives and employees alike.

There are various ways of ensuring that the work of consultative committees is not bogged down by trivia. Everyone involved should be made aware of the real purpose, objectives and scope of consultation through training and explanation. Representatives should be encouraged to think about whether the consultative committee is really the right forum for discussion of a particular point, and to talk this over with the person who has raised the point. The system should be structured such that all the members of a committee have enough in common in their work to be able to talk purposefully about their mutual tasks. Managers must take the trouble to put meaningful items for consultation on the agenda — if you do not bother doing this you have only yourself to blame if most of the committee's time is wasted on trivia. As a rough guideline, at least half of the consultative committee's time should be spent discussing management's points. If there are not enough management items on the agenda you are throwing away the chance for employees to be genuinely involved in decisions that affect them and, in many cases, to provide contributions that will improve those decisions. Moreover, if management defaults in this duty, the work of the committee will be perceived by the employees to be a charade — not a genuine consultation on important issues but simply a cosmetic exercise to make it *look* as if management is listening to the employees' views.

Policy decisions are not generally open to consultation (for example, they may involve confidential information), but the ways they are put into practice most certainly are. For example, some years back the decision was taken at senior level in British Home Stores to switch from weekly to monthly payment. There was no prior consultation on the decision itself, but later consultation produced many good ideas on how to implement it with the least possible disruption, staff unhappiness, difficulties in the accounts department, and so on. In fact, some of the best examples of successful consultation are to be found in the service industries, where managers can learn a great deal from the front-line staff who are dealing directly with customers.

Some of your decisions cannot be consulted because they have to be made immediately: it would be ridiculous to hang around for several weeks until the next meeting of the consultative committee. However, many of your decisions are *thinking* decisions: they benefit from being allowed time to mull over in your mind and from fruitful discussion with everyone involved — especially those who have to put them into practice. Also, there is no need to be too modest in the scope of the items you put forward for discussion: the chairman of one large organisation regularly inserts in the agendas of consultative committees the item 'If I were managing director for a day ...', and receives all sorts of useful ideas.

The overriding principle is that you should be seen to consult and to be committed to listening. The easiest way of achieving this is to be genuinely committed to the idea. If you are sincere about the whole exercise, your people will become likewise and, even if consultation produces few usable ideas, you will have vastly improved industrial relations within your organisation.

Making a success of it

To some managers consultation raises images of endless irrelevant meetings. To some employee representatives it is perceived as nothing more than a charade in which managements merely pretend that they are seeking employee involvement. Both viewpoints can be correct if consultation is mishandled.

Because the very word 'consultation' has this slightly unsavoury reputation (and 'committee' an even worse one!), you can increase the success of your consultative system simply by manipulating language. People who blanch at the thought of a 'consultative committee' may be much more positive if it is instead called a 'company advisory board', a 'joint participation group', or any other name that strikes you as appropriate. You might consult your employee representatives to see what *they* think would be a good title: they are possibly better equipped than you are to tell which combination of words will kindle the employees' enthusiasm. Getting the name right is especially important if you are trying to reestablish consultation after a first attempt has been allowed to fall by the wayside.

However, changing the terminology is really only a cosmetic aid: genuine progress in setting up or reestablishing consultation can come about only through concentrating on training and planning. Both managers and representatives should be trained to understand the objectives and limits of consultation, how to chair a meeting successfully, lead a discussion and present a case successfully, how to communicate with constituents, how to identify problems and work towards their solution, and how consultation can be fitted into the decision-making process. Last but not least, they should be trained to recognise what individuals can do to make consultation work.

Startlingly successful results have been achieved by many companies when they have trained managers and representatives alongside each other. This can break down many initial barriers, develop the group as a team, and give the group members the time and opportunity to look objectively at how, through working together, they can meet each other's expectations.

Another way of helping consultation work is to think about what is and what is not confidential information. All too often, managements work on the principle that everything is confidential until proved otherwise, which viciously restricts the number of topics that can be discussed by consultative committees. Of course, you have the right to be careful about what you disclose, and you have to follow the right procedure; for example, if you are putting hitherto 'confidential' information before the committee you must make sure that it is also communicated to all the relevant managers and supervisors. Also, for obvious reasons, it would be unfair of you to discuss matters in consultation meetings and then expect representatives not to pass them on to their constituents. There are exceptions to this rule: in certain circumstances you may find that representatives prefer to live with the natural discomfort of keeping information to themselves than to go without advance warning of impending decisions; redundancies are a prime example. Obviously, if the representatives can help you find a way of avoiding those redundancies, then everyone becomes a winner. However, such circumstances are the exception — that is, until the right atmosphere has been created by the repeated and regular use of consultation.

A related point is that you should have a procedure whereby managers are informed as soon as possible about decisions affecting them that have been brought about through consultations with employee representatives. Anyway, decisions should not be final until the relevant managers themselves have been consulted. It is vital that all managers concerned in the topics discussed in a consultative committee always receive copies of the minutes, preferably with points relevant to them highlighted in some way.

Procedures are important, so that everybody knows where they are, but if they are operated inflexibly you can lose a lot of useful feedback. You should try to be open about the agendas of the meetings, and allow representatives to bring up 'other matters'. If something comes up that cannot be sensibly discussed before further research, make sure it features on the agenda for the next meeting.

Never be tempted to offer financial incentives to people who volunteer to serve on consultative committees: the practice is fraught with difficulties, is certain to stir up resentments one way or the other, and will probably attract the wrong type of person. Consultation is done in company time and is a group effort; its benefits will affect everybody in the organisation — including those serving on the consultative committee — especially if there is some kind of bonus or profit-sharing scheme in operation.

Finally, for the system to work well, it must be regularly monitored. It is useful to ask committees themselves to analyse annually their own performances in terms of time, effort and resources. Such a self-assessment should include a look at the quality of communication with the front line, as well as a consideration of positive achievements.

The importance of successful consultation cannot be overestimated. Not only can it be helpful in producing good ideas for either the short or long term, it increases the involvement of the employees in their work. The more involved people are in their work, the more efficient the organisation becomes. As a delightful by-product, involvement enriches the lives of the people who work for you — and that should always be one of your primary objectives.

4 QUALITY CIRCLES AND SUGGESTION SCHEMES

Involvement of employees is, then, the key. We have discussed one important means of increasing involvement — the use of consultative committees. In this chapter we shall look at two other means whereby, through communication, you can further the process.

Quality circles are groups which meet regularly and voluntarily to identify and solve their own work-related problems and, with management approval, to implement their solutions.

Although the idea originated in the USA, quality circles were first used on a large scale in Japan. During the late 1940s Japanese industry began to realise that, if it was to compete with the large industrial nations, it had to make some radical reforms. Old ideas of management were discarded, and emphasis was placed on in-house training at shop-floor level; every effort went into passing more and more responsibility to the foreman and to the operator. Foremen were trained to be leaders — and also to spot quality problems in their work and encourage the people under them to do likewise.

The introduction, during the 1960s, of quality circles was a natural development. It is estimated that in Japan today there are more than a million quality circles, involving more than ten million workers. Since 1960, an annual 'National Quality Month' has been organised in the country to promote the idea of quality circles — the Japanese term for which translates literally as 'the gathering of the wisdom of the people'. The effectiveness of the practice can be gathered from the fact that, in 1980 alone, Toyota Motors received from its 46,000 workers no fewer than 587,000 suggestions to help improve quality and productivity.

In the mid-1970s industry in the USA began to show practical interest in quality circles, and many of the major companies there now use them — including such household 'names' as General Motors, Honeywell, Westinghouse and Lockheed. US industry had to accept that it would take much longer than in Japan for quality circles to gain general acceptance — they fit in much more easily with Japanese company and union structures, employee and management attitudes; and wages and incentive schemes — but progress has been steady. Even outside industry quality circles are now in extensive use in the USA: one example is the Mount Sinai Medical Center!

In the United Kingdom quality circles are being increasingly used: among the many major companies making use of them are British Leyland, Mullard, Marks & Spencer and May & Baker, and a number of US companies, including ITT, Honeywell and Tektronix, have introduced quality circles into their UK operations. What more and more UK companies, like their Japanese and US counterparts, have realised is that the initiative for improved quality must come from the shop floor.

Suggestion schemes are another major means of improving an organisation's efficiency from the bottom up. The earliest known suggestion scheme in industry was started at the Denny shipyard in Dumbarton, Scotland, in 1880, and several other British companies had followed suit by 1910. However, the spread of the idea in Britain has been rather slow: there are probably no more than about 500 suggestion schemes in existence in the country. However, to judge by an Industrial Society survey carried out in 1986, the number is now rapidly increasing.

The role of quality circles

Membership of quality circles should be entirely voluntary, and anyone wishing to join should be welcomed — just as anyone wishing not to take part should not be pressurised, as otherwise the person concerned is likely to be resentful and their membership counterproductive. There should be 6-12 people in each quality circle. If there are too many volunteers, either membership should become rotational or subgroups should be formed.

The supervisor or foreman should be the leader of the quality circle in his or her own work area. The supervisor's or foreman's role is to establish the circle by encouraging volunteers to set it up, and then to act as its chairperson or leader, because he or she is the member with the most training and experience. The leader guides the circle to make it cost-effective and to help it develop into a cohesive team that can tackle and solve quality and production problems.

Success of quality circles depends on the fact that employees feel that they are *theirs,* not just things set up to keep management happy. If you try to play too active a role, the best employee initiatives may well be lost. However, you should adopt a background supportive role, and possibly suggest topics for discussion. The major part you can play is to implement the idea of quality circles and then stand back. The managing director of one large printing company has stated his belief that quality circles worked for them in large part because 'I and my colleagues have been at particular pains not to interfere'.

Successful quality circles never develop into grumbling sessions or irrelevant discussions of grievances, and nor are they general chat sessions. The stress is always on the solving of problems and the production of action plans. Quality circles provide an opportunity for employees to suggest ways either of reducing costs or of improving quality of the product or service. Likely first choices for investigation are waste, machine and/or tool defects, and stock control. As the system matures, though, the quality circle will probably study also such areas as machine set-up time, productivity, material utilisation and handling, energy usage and safety. Circles must concentrate on practicalities rather than theories: they must aim to produce positive results and conclusions, not just woolly discussion.

Individual quality-circle members should start by listing what they see as potential problem areas. Then the group as a whole can establish priorities and seek solutions by drawing on the knowledge of its members and using simple problem-spotting and solution techniques. However, if technical and very detailed investigation is needed, management specialists may be asked to attend the circle's meetings. Otherwise, it is best to allocate one problem at a time for preliminary study by a subgroup consisting of those members most involved and knowledgeable in that particular area. Subgroup studies can usually be carried out between regular circle meetings; and often you will find that enthusiastic quality-circle supporters will devote much of their own time to problem-solving.

The role of quality circles is to

- brainstorm problems
- select the most relevant problem(s)
- have the circle investigate the problem(s)
- find solution(s) to the problem(s)

- take action, if the circle is authorised to do so, or
- make a presentation to management

Management must retain the power of final decision, but in many cases it makes sense to devolve authority to the quality circle so that problem-solving can be more rapidly effected. In other instances, the circle suggests and management has to decide. If the proposal is not accepted, then it is vital that management explains why not: failure to do so results in lost morale not just in the individual quality circle but in all the quality circles throughout the organisation.

Most of the time so far we have been talking about the application of the quality circle system to manufacturing industry, but circles also have a large part to play in the service industries. This is because they can be used to investigate all sorts of problems. For example, a large white-collar organisation found that staff in the typing pool suffered far too often from back pains, and many work-days were being lost as a result. During its very first meeting the company's quality circle decided to look into this problem, and it discovered that the chairs being used were not designed for typists. The quality circle made a recommendation to management, and this was speedily taken up. As a result, the problem was virtually eliminated and the organisation, obviously, became more efficient.

The question of when and where the quality circle should do its stuff is clearly an important one. Ideally, circles should meet once a week, during company time. The meetings should be conducted briskly for between thirty minutes and an hour. Regularity is important, since only through regularity will the work of the quality circle gain credibility. Dates for the meetings should be scheduled such that quality-circle members can put them in their diaries well in advance.

One obvious question is: How do quality circles fit in with team briefing (see Chapter 2) and consultative committees (see Chapter 3)?

It is important to realise that all three entities are quite different from each other. Although quality circles have a definite consultative role, they are really problem-solving sessions held by those who are actually at the 'cutting edge' of the job. The people who are contributing ideas are not representatives of their colleagues in any way, and have no obligation to report back to those colleagues; they are individual volunteers with individual ideas. Unlike the case of a consultative committee, management's role is never to tell a quality circle what its members should be discussing; management's contribution is, instead, to attend quality circle presentations and *listen* to those who have the most immediate experience of the practicalities of the job.

The benefits of quality circles

The financial benefits to the organisation through the use of quality circles can be astonishing, but they should never become paramount — otherwise, excessive strain is put on the circles to show immediate financial returns. Much more important is that the circles can give people tremendous satisfaction, and recognition for people's achievements. These things come about for three reasons: a greater feeling of team work, the increased involvement of individuals, and improvements in the way the task is carried out (and hence in the quality).

The development of team spirit through quality circles can have a dramatic influence on the atmosphere on the shop floor and throughout the company. Once quality circles are operating properly, you will find that there is soon a shift from a negative 'don't care' attitude to a positive desire to improve quality, reduce costs, and increase the effectiveness of efforts on the shop floor — even if the quality circles produce no ideas of particular value (although they almost always do). Clearly there is a latent interest in such matters among employees, who discover that through quality circles their dedication can be fulfilled rather than frustrated.

Such changes in attitude bear great fruits. Benefits are always hard to quantify, but reduction in absenteeism alone can bring substantial savings. Most sensible employers have long been seeking a way of involving people in their work, and this benefit is considered by many companies to be the greatest aim and achievement of quality circles — to the extent that, often, the savings and improvements in quality are regarded by managers as merely desirable side-effects!

Communication is also vastly improved by quality circles. Obviously communication between the members of the circle is improved, but there are also benefits to be derived both from lateral communication between circles operating in different work areas and from vertical communication between the shop floor and management. At the shop-floor level, quality circles can often bring together people who, even if working on the same line, have previously barely known each other: thanks to the circle, they not only discuss things together, they also act in concert. The circle also gives foremen a tremendous opportunity to develop their people as a team, working alongside them to identify and solve problems which everybody knew existed but which no one had ever been given the time or opportunity to deal with. Communication between circles can help reduce those tiresome situations whereby one part of an organisation doesn't know what the other is doing. The leaders of different circles can periodically hold 'leaders' meetings' to deal with the problem and to coordinate the work of their circles — again, such meetings help people to get to know each other, often for the first time, and much benefit can be reaped. And, in terms of vertical communication, quality circles clearly make a profound contribution to management's understanding of its own workforce. Managements are frequently astonished by the enthusiasm and knowledge of their employees, and the employees enjoy the opportunity of using their skills and seeing them put to full use.

So much for team considerations: what about the individual? Here again quality circles are invaluable in developing people's abilities. Supervisors gain not just from the training that quality circles involve, but also from the fact that the existence of the circle forces them to learn the leadership skills required to organise their teams. Those employees with most potential can be appointed by the supervisor to be subgroup leaders, thereby developing their leadership skills and providing an excellent supplementary means of training people for promotion. Finally, individuals within the circle begin to acquire and develop that 'critical eye' which alone can provide the productivity, quality and competitive edge that industry so sorely needs.

Finally, we can consider the benefits of quality circles in terms of the task and overall company viability.

Experience has graphically demonstrated that quality circles can do a great deal to improve productivity. Obviously the quality of the product has always been potentially an important factor in determining a company's market share but today, more than ever, when industry is facing such tough competition, sales are won through superior quality or lower costs. Effectiv e quality circles help effect both.

A 1978 government estimate was that about 15 per cent of the UK's turnover was being lost through inadequate quality. The causes were excessive scrap, inadequate machinery and tools, reworking, substandard inspections, and time and effort wasted in servicing defective products. Employees working on the job are already aware of defects, which they see every day and know to be serious, yet, because they are often given neither the time nor the opportunity to transmit the information to others, the faults are tolerated and continue uncorrected. The savings made through improving quality can be startling: in six months of 1980 they totalled more than half a million pounds for Rolls Royce.

Production costs, too, can be substantially affected by effective quality circles — for example, when employees recognise the massive problem of waste. Waste is most clearly seen by those on the shop floor, and it is there that solutions are most likely to be found. Other cost-saving aspects affected by quality circles include safety: there tend to be fewer accidents, because there is a general tightening up of discipline and procedures on the shop floor. Likewise, the reduction of absenteeism means money saved. Some of the savings involved may not in themselves be large, but a lot of small savings, added together, can come to a pretty impressive total.

Achieving commitment to quality circles

The most important thing to do before starting to set up quality circles is to ensure the full commitment of all the different elements within the organisation. To do this, it is vital that you make sure that the concept and aims of quality circles are fully understood by all concerned.

Management

When you are installing any new communication system, full and sincere management cooperation is of prime importance. Although not directly involved in the circles, management has an important part to play. Managers need to be persuaded not only to expend the time and money required for the circle meetings and preliminary training but also to make a firm personal commitment to supporting the scheme. They need to be convinced that quality circles will have a valuable effect on the atmosphere and attitudes within the company as a whole, as well as to direct quality and costs improvements.

Without this commitment the quality circles will fail; even worse, employees will become yet more frustrated. You, as a manager, must not just pay lip service to the idea: you must commit yourself to action. You must be ready to attend the circles' presentations, to listen with an open mind to the proposals, to consider them carefully and skilfully, and to carry through any that have merit. If any proposals are not adopted, you must explain in detail why not.

It is not always easy for management to take on these obligations, but it is essential if your scheme of quality circles is to prosper. As the personnel manager of one West Midlands company which failed to achieve a quality-circle system put it succinctly: 'All you need is one pig-headed manager and any effort to motivate the circle is dead.' Make sure that you are not that pig-headed manager, and then make sure that none of your colleagues is, either.

How do you go about getting the commitment?

The first move is to arrange a management presentation. This is best done by someone from outside the group who has professional credibility. A 1986 survey carried out by The Industrial Society of over 127 organisations showed that 73.3 per cent had opted for the use of an external consultant (the most frequently cited advisors being The Industrial Society itself and David Hutchins). Although detailed data on failed quality-circle systems were not available, the researchers were convinced that the use of outside assistance in establishing the system was a major factor in ensuring that it lasted. So, although outside consultants do not come cheap, it probably makes a lot of sense to make the investment.

During the management presentation, the philosophy and merits of quality circles can be fully explained, questions from managers can be answered, and any reservations can be dealt with. It is also useful to mention specific areas within the organisation where quality circles can be expected to have the most impact.

There will always be some managers who are not initially prepared to make the commitment. So long as these are in the minority and do not intend to take positive steps to disrupt the introduction of the scheme, you can hope it won't matter too

53

much. However, most companies have found that managers have been frankly amazed and delighted by the sheer professionalism and quality of even the first presentations made to them by their quality circles, and thereafter enthusiasm has been contagious.

Almost exactly one third of the organisations sampled in The Industrial Society survey cited management resistance as a serious difficulty in installing quality circles — indeed, it was the most frequently cited problem. So make sure that the presentation to management is as effective as it can be.

Unions

Contrary to the suspicions of the more paranoid managers, most union leaders echo Terry Duffy's remarks: 'Skilfully installed, quality circles can only improve the lot of employees. I whole-heartedly support them.'

A meeting with the unions should follow the initial presentation made to management, and should, once again, explain the idea and benefits of quality circles, and be carried out by the same professional third party. After the presentation, it is extremely likely that the unions will give their commitment to the idea. The only known times when quality circles have failed because of union opposition is when managements have sought to bypass the unions in installing the scheme.

Never give credence to the picture of the brutish, uncooperative shop steward portrayed in all too many regions of the popular press. Of course, there are pig-headed shop stewards just as there are pig-headed managers, but most shop stewards will easily give their commitment to the scheme in the belief that any *honest* effort to involve the workforce more closely in the activities of the company can only improve the lot of their members. You may find the occasional shop steward who is wary at first, but almost without exception, as soon as he or she sees how quality circles are run by *volunteers* from the shop floor, and how management has only a listening role, acceptance will be total.

All the company

The last step is the making of a presentation to the company, division, unit or department where it is intended to start the system up. As before, you need to ensure complete understanding of the objectives of quality circles, but another aim of the presentation is to establish in which parts of the company the first circles should be inaugurated. Unless this latter aim is achieved, it is possible that your system of quality circles will never properly get off the ground. And unless the objectives are completely understood by all, it is possible that the system will be misjudged and misunderstood by those members of the workforce who do not volunteer to take part, and who will believe that the quality circles are merely another tool of the bosses. However, if you do your best to make the system a success, most disbelievers will come round when they see the positive contribution the circles are making to life on the shop floor.

Making quality circles work

Experience has shown that there are three main factors that determine the success of quality circles:

- the quality of the scheme's coordinator (sometimes called its facilitator) and his or her dedication in agreeing to put aside a substantial amount of time in order to make the system work
- the training given to both circle leaders and circle members — this must be carefully and skilfully done if the circle is to start off on the right lines
- the willingness and commitment of all of management to make the scheme work (as we have already discussed)

One person should be trained as the coordinator of the scheme. He or she should be utterly committed to its success. The person's roles are in the following areas:

- Training. Once all the presentations have been made and it has been established in which areas of the company quality circles will be introduced, the supervisors involved need guidance and training.
- Assisting the leaders. Without interfering in any way, the coordinator should sit in on the circles' initial meetings, helping the leader to establish the right atmosphere and fix aims, to convince any members who are still a bit dubious, and to suggest some of the first problems that could be tackled — in other words, to get the show on the road.
- Coordination. He or she may need, for example, to organise an ancillary quality circle to get together on problems that involve several work areas with mutual interests, and to invite

specialists to join in a quality-circle meeting to help solve a particular technical problem — although these specialists will have attended the initial company presentation, they will probably need specific supplementary briefing before being brought along to the quality circle.

- To serve as a link with management. The coordinator must ensure that the circle adequately reports its activities to management and also that management does not interfere too much with the work of the circle and thereby jeopardise its independence. Above all the coordinator must ensure that managers seriously and sincerely consider the presentations made to them by the quality circles.

Who should the coordinator be? Because a large part of his or her role is involved in training, it is often a good idea to opt for the training manager. This approach has proved most successful when the training manager is someone who has also had line experience. Above all, he or she must be a person who inspires trust and who is at ease with management and employees alike. The coordinator must have the ability to be a leader but, although able to stimulate people, he or she must be sensible enough to resist any temptation to take over the scheme or to dominate the circle leaders.

Training, as noted, is vital. Successful quality circles serve as a catalyst to release knowledge which is already there. The challenge is to find ways of training employees to spot problems, and to show them how to organise their thoughts and to think through possible technical difficulties and alternatives in order to put their ideas into practice.

A comprehensive training programme will probably require first a three-day course (organised by outside specialists) for the circle leaders, followed by a one-day course, or two half-day ones, for circle members.

Each leader needs to be trained to set up and manage a quality circle in his or her own area. At the start, careful and close control will be required, but the leader must not be encouraged to overpower the members of the circle and thereby stifle their opinions. Leaders must be trained to acquire a full understanding of all the ins and outs of quality circles, because they must be fully equipped to sell the idea and to enthuse all their people with it. Other items involved in the leader's training are the ability to hold effective meetings (see Chapter 7), basic management techniques (for example, the use of statistics), and the best ways of making presentations to management so that the quality circle's proposals are more likely to be taken up.

The training of circle members is best done in conjunction with that of the leaders, and should include a detailed introduction to quality circles, information on the techniques needed to run them, and examples of practical diffulties that may arise while the scheme is being put into practice.

Why use suggestion schemes?

Like quality circles, suggestion schemes are a means of upward communication whereby the ideas and knowledge of the people actually doing the job can be conveyed to management.

Why are suggestion schemes necessary? Why should even efficient and successful organisations go to the trouble of setting them up? And, if the employees' ideas are rejected, will this not generate ill-feeling and accusations of unfairness?

To answer the last question first, there are indeed circumstances where suggestion schemes can make a bad working atmosphere worse. However, the evidence is clear that they can be of real value to management. This comes about because of two factors: they improve employee relations and they help productivity. (A minor by-product is that suggestion schemes can be good for public relations: the media quite often pick up stories about the implementation of employees' suggestions.)

Let us look at the employee-relations factor first.

A suggestion scheme should be a two-way communication channel, with ideas — good or bad — flowing upward and with a steady stream of information flowing downward, so that people know why their ideas have been accepted or rejected and gain a better insight into the organisation and its inner workings. As with quality circles, the most important thing is that people know that their thinking powers are being utilised, and that they are being encouraged to make a positive contribution to the organisation's progress. At the very least, people know they have a way of approaching management on subjects that previously they would have kept to themselves.

The trend towards functional specialisation has in many industries tended to take away from employees all responsibility for thinking about their job, planning it, and using their imagination. Suggestion schemes act to reverse this trend: they enlarge the job and give back to the individual a means of self-expression. True, this may be of value to only a minority of employees, but that minority can be a significant one.

In small organisations, the case for suggestion schemes is not so pressing, because contact between management and employees is likely to be close. Likewise, in organisations with a high proportion of skilled employees, there will probably already be suitable channels of communication. However, the larger the organisation, the more likely it is that it would benefit from the use of suggestion schemes.

From a management point of view, a suggestion scheme can help create a cost-conscious labour force which will learn to cooperate with, rather than resist, change. It can be used to pinpoint people whose talents may have gone unnoticed, and it can also — along with others of the communication systems we discuss in this book — tell you about the current climate of opinion at all levels and in all departments of your organisation.

Improving productivity is the more obvious and tangible function of a suggestion scheme. In fact, assuming your organisation's management is competent, the increased profitability brought about by the suggestions will individually be small — unless, of course, an employee comes up with some really startling idea, in which case he or she should already have been talent-spotted by management. However, as we noted on page 52, a lot of small contributions add up to a big one. In 1986 The Industrial Society carried out research into suggestion schemes in various companies, and discovered that 91 companies had on average saved about £87,000 each during 1985 through the use of suggestion schemes. Two, IBM UK plc and Lucas Industries Ltd, had saved well over £800,000 each in that year.

Which of the two factors — employee relations or productivity — makes the bigger contribution depends on the nature of the business. In smaller companies, the improvement in employee morale may be more significant, whereas in the mass-production industries productivity savings that are small in percentage terms can mean the saving of hundreds of thousands of pounds each year.

Management support

As with quality circles, the key to successful implementation of a suggestion scheme is management support. Active encouragement from senior managers is vital: this sets the pace for the equally active cooperation of everyone else involved. But you should not regard the scheme, however much you support it, as a panacea: the most ardent supporters of suggestion schemes recognise that they should be only an adjunct to existing management methods for improving employee relations and increasing productivity.

Moreover, you have to take care that the structure of your particular suggestion scheme is tailored to the needs of your organisation — otherwise you can simply breed discontent. It is hopeless to expect a suggestion scheme to sit comfortably in an organisation where employees are not in other ways encouraged to express their views. It is probably even more futile to expect suggestions to make any progress at all in an organisation in which production, technical and service departments are working at cross purposes. It may be, though, that a well founded and administered scheme can in itself be instrumental in bringing about the very conditions in which it and the organisation can flourish, but the magnitude of the task facing the scheme in such circumstances should not be underestimated.

If management backing is lukewarm, even the appointment of a full-time administrator will not prevent the failure of a suggestion scheme. Backing is most important in the early days; after a while (perhaps a few years) the suggestion scheme will become such a fact of life that its existence will no longer provoke opposition.

One important reason why such opposition can come about is that managers feel threatened: they regard suggestions in their own spheres of operation as implied criticisms, especially if those suggestions are then acted upon. This is where senior management has an important role. It must make it clear that it holds the less senior managers in esteem not just for the ideas they themselves produce but also for their ability to elicit ideas from their subordinates, and to recognise a good idea when they see it.

Inevitably there will be teething troubles. Few managers have time on their hands, and one can in a way sympathise if, faced with severe pressure of work, you are impatient of the time you have to spend on something that may well prove to be trivial or useless. However, if you are secure in the knowledge that top management attaches great importance to the scheme, and that your position is in no way being undermined, the difficult situations should be few and far between.

Selling the scheme

Although good administration of the scheme (see below) is probably the best insurance against failure, there can be no doubt of the importance of positive publicity in maintaining the employees' interest and improving their response. The first difficulty for the administrator is to persuade management that a suggestion scheme will not succeed unless its potentials and achievements are constantly placed before the employees.

Of the numerous publicity methods available. the two most obvious are the house magazine (see Chapter 6) and the poster. The house magazine is probably the more potent. Employees who read of awards given to colleagues are immediately stimulated to submit ideas of their own; moreover, since the magazine is delivered to the employee's home, there is a much higher chance that he or she will actually read it. Note, though, that such publicity needs to be regular if the level of response is to be maintained. One organisation periodically incorporates a suggestion form into its house journal and finds this always increases the flow of suggestions.

The role of posters is a little more difficult to analyse. They are certainly one of the commonest forms of publicity used, and they serve to keep a scheme in the employees' eyes. Also, the *absence* of posters has a definite adverse effect on a scheme. You should make every attempt to ensure that the posters are attractive, and obviously their positioning is important. In some organisations a special notice-board giving details of results is effective. Should a suggestion not have been accepted, it is obviously best to omit the name of the person who made the suggestion.

Attractive illustrated booklets can be issued to all employees giving an outline of the scheme. These should be clear, simple and well designed. A number of other techniques that have proved useful are pay-packet inserts, annual award winners' dinners, and special directors' awards for exceptional ideas.

Competitions, too, can be used to stimulate interest. They can operate between departments or between sites, or recognise the best suggestion of the month in the field of safety, quality, or whatever. Some companies give an award for the Best Suggestion of the Year. An interesting variation is the Best Suggestor of the Year award for the person who has had most suggestions accepted. Some organisations operate lotteries or prize draws in order to encourage employee participation. However you go about it, continual publicity is of paramount importance if you are to ensure a high level of employee participation — essential if your suggestion scheme is to be successful.

You may find that a long-running scheme is faltering and needs revitalisation. If so, it might be easier and more cost-effective to start a new scheme than to try to revive one in which everybody has lost faith. This is a drastic move, but it may be worth it. Organisations that have successfully followed this route in the last few years have included British Airways, British Telecom, and London Underground.

An individual interview to explain why a suggestion cannot be adopted, and the willingness to admit mistakes and deal fairly with appeals, will increase the confidence of employees in the justice of the suggestion scheme. This is something which is much easier to achieve in smaller organisations, but it is certainly far from impossible to achieve in larger ones.

If your organisation includes a formal communication system such as team briefing (see Chapter 2), it may be worth channelling information about suggestion schemes through this route: the number of awards received, the level and number of awards, the total amount paid out by the organisation, and so on. Such a practice is particularly beneficial in large organisations.

One final thing must be stressed: the personal touch, to convince employees that you (and the organisation) are handling their ideas sympathetically. This is worth columns of written matter in the house journal or a whole series of first-class posters.

Eligibility for awards

In an ideal world employees' enthusiasm for suggestion schemes would continue without the need for some kind of financial incentive, but in the real world an award structure is required.

An award structure is not an end in itself. It is a means to serve, first as a way of justly rewarding people whose ideas have been accepted, and second as a means of encouraging continued support for the suggestion scheme. The award structure should not be rigid: if the suggestion scheme shows signs of failing, the award structure should be modified.

What is a just reward for a good idea? There is no easy answer, but two points are worth noting:

- where possible, awards should be based on calculable savings, and the employees should be provided with the basis of that calculation
- if it is impossible to calculate the savings, some kind of points system, rewarding features such as originality and ingenuity, may be used to ensure consistency of approach

The question of eligibility is often a source of some controversy. Essentially, as few employees as possible should be excluded from the award scheme, although, of course, what is possible in one organisation may be impossible in another. As a general rule, you should always include all manual workers and, after that, as many nonmanual workers as is practicable. However, lines of eligibility differ greatly between organisations. Some firms exclude all staff personnel; others include office staff but exclude all managers and supervisors; and yet others include everyone but give no reward where the suggestion could be considered to form a part of the employee's 'normal duties and responsibilities'.

This last obviously makes it necessary that management are clear on exactly what the 'normal duties and responsibilities' of the employee *are* — or, more accurately, were at the time the suggestion was made. Managements are often far from clear on this, so that any problems arising are not so much ones of eligibility as ones of job specification. Once an employee's terms of reference have been clarified, it is usually reasonably simple for a committee to decide whether an award is justifiable.

There are two fundamental questions:

- could the idea be implemented without reference to a senior manager or without the approval of a technical department?
- would suggestors be open to criticism from their seniors for not having put forward the idea as part of their normal work?

If the answer to both questions is 'no', then the suggestion is outside the scope of the suggestor's 'normal duties and responsibilities'.

Whenever the eligibility of suggestors is genuinely in doubt, they should, without hesitation, be given the benefit of that doubt. The money spent on the award will be easily earned back in terms of the goodwill created, which will in turn generate further support for the suggestion scheme. If you are stingy in cases like this, the employees will begin to regard the scheme as nothing more than a management fraud — and, in a way, they will be right.

In some firms supervisory staff and/or members of certain technical departments are excluded, and instead participate in special schemes. In other firms they are included in the main scheme but are not eligible for rewards — on the basis that the scheme gives imaginative or keen employees the opportunity to show their qualities, which in a large organisation might well otherwise go unnoticed.

One rule for awards is worth considering. For some while after the introduction of new equipment or procedures, there may very well be teething troubles. It is legitimate to suggest that, for a certain period after the change, no suggestions on that subject will be eligible for an award. Of course, you may lose your organisation a lot of money on occasion, because a brilliant suggestion may be lost in administrative staff time to sort out the teething troubles themselves, rather than let other employees jump the gun.

Lastly, you must consider the eligibility of employees who have resigned, been fired, or even died. The cardinal principle is that it is the *date of the suggestion* which counts, not the date of the award: not only will your apparent generosity be good for PR, you will avoid any possibility of a damaging and expensive lawsuit should someone, quite fairly, sue you for having swiped his or her idea.

In general, problems of eligibility are rarely difficult. They can usually be settled by an analysis of the person's job and, thereafter, by precedent. As noted, however, if in doubt always err on the side of generosity.

5 REPORT WRITING

Most of us find that putting words on paper is hard work, and often we are doubtful about whether the end-product justifies all the time and effort. When we are busy, we tend to resent 'wasting time' writing reports. But writing reports is as important a part of our job as maintaining production levels or improving staff relations — in fact, it can help us do both.

Effective writing requires skill: it does not require artistry. This skill can be learned. In this chapter we shall give a few guidelines, which ought to be enough for you to acquire something of the art of report writing. If you want to take matters further, there are a number of books on how to write, but these are often of dubious value; one published a few years ago was called *How to Write 'How To' Books!* You are better off going to evening classes in creative writing, such as those run by The Workers' Educational Association, where professional writers will give you the benefit of their experience. Alternatively, you could take a correspondence course, but these are expensive.

However, for the sort of basic writing skills you require to produce a report, the information given in this chapter should be enough.

The function of a report can be one, several or all of the following:

- to act as a communicator of ideas or information
- to influence decision making
- to initiate action
- to serve as a persuader

In all of these cases, the role of the report is not to be the *end* of a process but the *beginning* of a new one. The report is a vital link in the chain of action, and is essential to the successful functioning of any organisation.

What is a report?

The necessary components of a report are five in number. A good report requires a subject, a writer, a reader, a structure and a purpose — forget any of these at your peril. The overriding consideration is that the report must *communicate*. It must be persuasive, decisive and action-centred. If you bear in mind the five primary components, the rest should follow naturally.

So, how do you set about writing a report? As with any other task, the first thing you must do is *plan:* you must work out how much time the job will take, how you can relate this to the rest of your workload, and how the time available for writing the report should be allocated.

The last of these considerations is the most important: given that you never seem to have enough time anyway, how can the time that you have available be used to best advantage? The answer is to apportion the time by breaking the task down into its components. Writing a report involves a number of quite separate activities. If you have it clearly in your mind what these are you can deal with them step by step, giving to each of them an appropriate amount of time. Doing this reduces the task to manageable proportions and saves the effort that would be wasted were you to go about the chore in a haphazard way.

In this chapter we shall look at a method of report-writing which, if you agree with it, you should stick to and apply consistently. If you wish to use a different method, fair enough; but stick to that, and apply it consistently too. The method discussed here breaks the task of report-writing down into three main sections, each of which is in turn divided into three 'activities'. The breakdown looks like this:

- before
  - writer
  - reader
  - material
- writing
  - structure
  - language
  - presentation
- after
  - typing
  - revision
  - final check

As we have hinted, there are other plans of attack, but this one has the merit that it is known to work, so if you have no particular reason for going about things in some other way, you would be as well to follow this scheme.

The three-point programme: before

You, as writer, may feel that time spent at this stage is wasted, but in fact it is the best investment of your resources that you can make. The main purpose of this preparatory stage is to force you to decide *what* you're going to write about and *why*. There are three factors to be considered at this early stage: the writer (you), the reader and the material.

The writer

Why are you writing the report? Ideally, because you are the best person to do the job. Either you are the expert in possession of the necessary facts or you are the person best equipped to unearth them.

The next thing to determine is the true subject of the report. You have to discuss your terms of reference with whoever it is who requires the report, and make sure you are both in agreement about them: it is a good idea to set down the agreed terms, and make sure the other person has a copy. Also, you must establish the report's purpose: you have to know why you are writing as well as what you are supposed to be writing about. Of course, the facts you report will remain the same, but the way you use them will be determined by the report's overall purpose. The better you understand the purpose, the better you will be able to communicate the message. You will be able to make the *significant* facts stand out from the general background of information, so that your readers will know on what they should act and why.

The reader

Before you start to produce your report, think about the reader. The reader is the other end of the communication chain. If you produce a brilliant report, but one that is not tailored for the people who are expected to read it, you are wasting your time — and theirs. Imagine that you are *speaking* to the people who will be reading your report: obviously you would tailor a speech to the audience, so do the same when writing for a readership. You have to focus the attention of your readers by directing it to their particular needs, interests and requirements, but also you have to write it in the kind of language they will understand.

For example, the contents of a company's annual report can be used and presented in many different ways. The shareholders will want it written one way, the directors another; employees and consumers should have the information presented in yet further different ways. So *think* about your readers: if you do not, you will almost inevitably fail to communicate effectively.

The material

To compile a report you need, clearly, to gather information. If you go about this in a hit-and-miss way you will waste a lot of time. You need to be methodical, and the best way of doing this is constantly to bear in mind the report's purpose. The first step is to get all your ideas of what could be in the report onto paper. Take a plain sheet of paper and write the main theme of the report in the middle of it. Write down all the ideas and thoughts you have on the subject, starting from the central focus and branching out along the lines of connecting ideas. Don't worry too much about organisation at this stage: just let your ideas flow freely. Once you have got everything down on the paper, you can start organising your ideas by circling any related sections and establishing your order of priorities.

With complicated reports — or reports prepared over a long period — it is often helpful to draw up a more elaborate plan based on the notes you have made. One scheme is to use a 'column plan'. You draw up four columns on a sheet of paper. Working from left to right, you set down information in the following four categories:

- items for investigation and topics to be covered: 'What do I need to know?'
- sources: 'Where do I find the information?'
- visual material: 'What visual materials do I need?'
- arrangement of material: 'In what order should I present my material?'

Using the column plan all through the preparatory stage of your report, you will build up a complete picture in each area as you progress, which is much better than trying to collect your ideas at the last minute from scattered notes and half-baked impressions.

Once your ideas are in order, you should decide on your conclusions and recommendations, and note these at the bottom of your column plan. Until you have decided on these, you cannot begin the task of actually writing the report, because of course the final version will be coloured by what you want the report to say. Also, it is at this early stage that you are most fully in possession of the facts; later, through misremembering something, you may draw the wrong conclusions from your researches.

From your complete findings, select only sufficient material to support your arguments. Too much information will simply overload the reader; although, by contrast, too little will make it look as if you are basing your argument on insufficient evidence. You have to find the right balance. The easiest way to do this is to consider both the purpose of the report and the requirements of its readers. Imagine that *you* are the intended reader, and try to think what you would hope to get from the report.

Another thing to do before you start writing is to arrange the order of presentation of each section, as well as the order within each section of the items to be discussed. The most logical order, in both cases, is usually the one which the reader will be able to follow most clearly. Work out headings for each section and subsection: headings are signposts to the reader, but they are also signposts to you as you write the report.

The three-point programme: writing

When you are writing your report there are three main considerations: structure, language and presentation. A combination of a sound framework, a clear style and an attractive appearance will encourage the reader to study the report and will make it easier to understand.

Structure

A good structure for your report might be:

- title page
- contents

- summary
- introduction
- findings
- conclusions
- recommendations
- appendices
- acknowledgements/references/bibliography
- index (only for long reports)

Most of these items are self-explanatory, so here we shall look only at the four most important ones: the introduction, your findings, your conclusions and your recommendations.

In the *introduction* you 'tell them what you're going to tell them' — that is, you lead the reader into the report. Here is not the place for detail: that will be provided in the 'findings' section. Although it is presented as a separate section, the introduction should form a coherent whole with the next two sections. You may prefer to state your terms of reference before the introduction proper, or you may prefer to include them here. In either event, the introduction should state

- the authorising person or body requesting the report
- the author or group responsible for the investigation
- the purpose or reason for the report
- the method of enquiry — that is, sources and the form of enquiry used
- explanation of the arrangement and grouping of the data presented in the rest of the report
- general background to the report's subject — just enough to enable the reader to understand and follow the report

In the *findings* section you present all your material — both the facts you have discovered and the information you have drawn from them. The material in this section provides the foundation for the next two sections, your conclusions and your recommendations.

If your findings are lengthy and/or complex, you might find it useful, both for yourself and for the reader, to end each subsection with its own conclusion. These can then be gathered, restated and analysed later in the report.

In the *conclusions* section you 'tell them what you have told them'; in a long report it will probably be a summary of all the various conclusions you have presented in the 'findings' section. Normally, this section shows the writer for the first time drawing together all the threads of his or her report.

No new information should appear here: you are considering the evidence presented in your 'findings' section and coming to a conclusion based on it.

The *recommendations* section is the 'action centre' of your report.

Your recommendations should follow naturally from your conclusions. They should offer a solution to any problem or fulfil any requirement implied in your terms of reference. They should meet your own defined purpose in compiling the report. They should persuade the reader that the action recommended is essential, and convince him or her that such action is practicable.

Language

The best maxim if you are in doubt about how to express something in written form is to say it, and then write down what you have said. This is your report, and so it should be written in your words, not in some archaic, over-formalised language which you regard as 'proper' English. There is no such thing as 'proper' English: there is only *good* English.

How do we assess what is good English? Well, by the success with which it carries out its particular function. When you are writing a report, the function of the language you use is to communicate. Take this as your criterion and you should not go too far wrong.

Remember, the ability to write well is a skill that can be learned, not a talent given to you by some capricious muse. The quality of the words you use reflects the quality of your thinking, and also affects it. Poor writing is often a sign of muddled ideas; and once you have expressed your ideas in a form that other people can understand you usually find that the muddle has been sorted out.

You are writing to communicate, not to mystify or impress. Focus on the specific purpose you have in mind — in other words, keep to the point. Remember also that you have a definite reader, and direct your writing towards that reader. Doing so establishes the right 'tone of voice' in your writing, and helps you keep your writing closer to the spoken word. Do not write for an amorphous mass of readers 'out there': 'speak onto paper' for a single reader.

(This is what I am trying to do in this book, for example.)

Try to make sure your choice of words is accurate, and that the words really mean what you think they mean. To choose a mundane example, a lot of people use the word 'infer' when they mean 'imply'. In most instances this does not matter much, but sometimes it can create major misunderstandings. On the same tack, avoid jargon — not only can it be incomprehensible, it can seriously mislead, because jargon terms can mean radically different things to different people — and be careful about your use of abbreviations and acronyms. Do not use them too often, and always ensure that they are spelled out in full the first time they appear in the report.

Brevity and clarity are important qualities in your writing. You might think that 'at this particular moment in time' is more impressive than 'now', but your readers will just think you are being pompous — especially if they have to wade through hundreds of pretentious phrases like that during the course of your report. Yes, of course you can allow your writing to become expansive if there is a good reason — there is no harm in popping in the odd joke, for example — but in general you should be as brief as you can be without producing a constipated screed of compressed opacity.

Clarity goes hand in hand with brevity. To be clear, your writing must be definite; it must allow no room for misunderstanding. This means you must know precisely what you want to say — in other words, the facts — and not allow yourself to hide any gaps in your knowledge behind vague generalisations. If you say, for example, 'a certain amount of money', that could mean anything from threepence to £5,000 (or much more). If you can, specify the amount of money; if you cannot, at least try to give the reader some idea of the sort of sum you are talking about. Another point in connection with clarity is that you should use short, simple, easily understandable words rather than long, 'impressive' ones — you should try to find things out, not 'endeavour to ascertain' them. Also, very often those 'impressive' words do not mean what you think they do. For example, people often write 'utilise' because they thinks it looks better than 'use', but in fact the two words have subtly different meanings.

In your writing, be active rather than passive, and personal rather than impersonal: both qualities enhance the clarity of your writing, as well as making it more readable. You've probably had one of those letters from the Inland Revenue which begins 'The

Inspector of Taxes has received your communication of the 19th inst. ...': what the writer is really trying to say is 'Thanks for your letter of the 19th ...'. The passive, impersonal approach of the bureacratic letter is something which it is all too easy to adopt in your own writing, so beware of it — not just because it sends your readers to sleep but because it allows you to avoid the responsibility for making definite statements in your report. If you find you really want to shrug off that responsibility, then you should never make the statements in the first place.

Finally, as in other areas of communication, use examples to help you present your argument. A simple example can convey as much as pages of tightly reasoned abstract theory. For instance, in the previous paragraph I used as an example a few words from a letter produced by the Inland Revenue. The alternative would have been to spend a page and a half explaining why passive, impersonal writing turns readers off.

Presentation

A lot of people think that presentation is 'just a case of window dressing' — but go to a high-street shop and ask the people there how important they think window dressing is. Good presentation will not, in the end, disguise the fact that a report is badly researched and written; but if your report is shoddily presented people may never get around to reading it. You must make people want to read your report, and good presentation is one of the most important ways through which you can do this.

If you still do not believe me, ask yourself why the publishers of this book spent so much money giving it an attractive jacket, good typography, pleasing paper ... Yes, they did it because they believed the money was well spent — that the attractive presentation would make you more likely to want to read, and therefore buy, this book.

Layout is important. The typing should be double-spaced, and the page-margins should be wide. There is some debate about how often you should use headings and subheadings — some people say to use them liberally, while other people say that to do so is just a way of masking sloppy writing and, hence, sloppy thinking. In this book, aside from chapter headings, there are only two 'weights' of subheading. If you find that in a 5,000-word report you want to use more than this, then you should think pretty carefully about what you are doing. Whatever system of subheadings you use, make sure it's consistent. The same applies if you decide it would be useful to number the headings.

The three-point programme: after

Once the first draft of your report has been written, force yourself to forget about it for at least a day or two — preferably three weeks — before you attempt to do any more work on it: when you come back to it with a fresh eye you will be much better equipped to judge it. One way of making sure this happens is to send the draft off for typing.

Typing

There are many advantages to having your first draft typed up. When it comes back, all neat and tidy, it is a different animal: it has an air of confidence and authority it did not have before, and that will help boost your own confidence in it. At the same time, you will find it much easier to be critical about your own work: you can be much more objective about it, for some reason. Finally, it is much easier to do your revisions on a clean typescript than on your original version, which is probably looking a bit of a mess by now, with crossings-out, transpositions, and the like.

Brief the typist carefully, and if possible try to get him or her *involved* in the work. You are much more likely to get a good result if you speak with the typist personally than if you simply put your original into the typing pool's in-tray.

If possible, find someone who uses a word processor. It is obviously a waste of effort to type out the whole report twice when, using a word processor, the business of inserting the revisions becomes pretty trivial. Another advantage is that if, when you get the final version, you spot a typing error, it is comparatively simple to amend this on a word processor whereas, if the person is using a typewriter, either the whole page has to be retyped or the amendment has to be done by hand.

Revision

When you receive the typed version of your first draft you should read it over from beginning to end. That is the only way you will get any 'feel' of the report's overall impact — the way it will strike the reader. As you read, mark the passages that require attention.

Afterwards, come back to these passages and deal with them. Then, finally, you can begin the task of detailed revision.

You may find it a good idea, before sending the report off for final typing, to have a colleague read it and discuss it with you. Once you have incorporated any useful revisions he or she may have suggested, the document is ready. Brief the typist carefully to make sure that all details of layout, headings, house-style and so on are fully understood.

Final check

When you get the final version, make a point of proofreading it. Even the best of typists can make mistakes, and what the worst of typists can do is painful even to contemplate. One obvious point which a lot of people miss is that you should check that everything is there: typists quite frequently miss out sentences, paragraphs, or even entire pages.

The gentle art of précis

Whatever you call it — abstract, digest, precis, summary — somewhere in the report, usually at the beginning, there should be a brief statement of the chief points. This should remain faithful to the original, cover *all* the essential points, and be fully comprehensible in its own terms — not just in the context of the full document.

The précis may serve any or all of these functions:

- an introduction to the subject of the full report
- a guide to readers as to whether the report is of any interest to them
- a time-saver for busy executives: often initial decisions are based on a reading of the summary plus an examination of the recommendations
- for you, a check that in the report you have actually said what you intended to say

Whether the précis you are providing is of your own work or of someone else's, the following routine should help you:

- read the whole document
- isolate and summarise its central theme
- study the document section by section

- eliminate from the précis all repetitions, lists, examples and detailed descriptions amd replace them with generalised statements: your aim is to give an overview, not to convey the detail
- read through your précis to ensure that it gives a fair impression of the original and will make sense to someone who cannot or will not read the full report

Your first report is always the most difficult. It may seem that we have talked about a lot of points that you are supposed to remember, but after you have written a couple of reports you won't even need to think about them: they will be more-or-less instinctive to you. As long as you bear in mind that your prime task in writing a report is to communicate information, you should find little trouble.

6 HOUSE JOURNALS AND OTHER EMPLOYEE REPORTS

House journals — probably the most frequently encountered way by which management reports to the employees — are important channels whereby you cannot just communicate news about company activities and successes but also *motivate* the employees. Those employees want to know what is going on — indeed, they have every right to — and so it is up to you to make sure that they do. The more they understand the organisation's current position, the less likely it is that different employees and even departments will unwittingly work at cross-purposes.

House journals came about because companies grew bigger. It became difficult — or even impossible — for managers to talk to all their people during a half-hour's brisk walk, even if they wanted to. Just as important, communications between different parts of the organisation broke down: the topics of gossip in the packing room — such as who had just won a sports contest, or whatever — were unknown to the people in the machine room. Gossip like this may not seem especially relevant to the task in hand, but in fact it is all part of what keeps an organisation flourishing. In the same vein, because managers so rarely communicated with the workers, they began to think of those workers as nothing more than names and numbers — something which the workers sensed and, quite justifiably, resented. Many damaging disputes over the years could have been prevented had managements communicated properly that they valued their employees as people.

Some organisations, as they grew larger, simply ignored the problem. In Britain, however, the Great Western Railway recognised the difficulty and turned to the press — in the form of the house journal — to circumvent it. In the mid-1880s the same idea began to flourish in the United States, and in 1895 William Lever, one of the most forward-looking of industrialists, summarised the problem and its solution in his editorial in the first issue of *Port Sunlight Monthly:* '... the only alternative is to call to our aid the power of the Press.'

Since Lever's day the reasons for publishing house journals have varied, and not always have they been good ones. Sometimes it has been nothing more than companies keeping up with the Joneses; other times it has been a question of spending a lot of money in order to produce a glossy publication just so that it will look good on the receptionist's desk. But in the decades since World War II directors, managers and unions have come increasingly to rely upon house journals as media for communication up, down and sideways.

Other employee reports serve much the same function, although they tend more to be a tool whereby information is communicated down than do house journals. They contain more formal items (although they need not be formally presented), such as the chairman's annual message. Also, because they tend to be less frequent — usually annual — many companies are prepared to be more lavish in their presentation, opting for wall-to-wall colour in printed material, producing videos or films, or using expensive studio staff and time to produce sound cassettes. In this chapter we shall concentrate primarily on house journals, bearing in mind that in most instances the comments apply equally to other forms of employee reports.

Ways and means

House journals have been the subject of many pointing fingers and unfavourable surveys in recent years. One commentator says they are not as good as briefing groups, another that they are little better than notice-boards, while a third claims that, in these days of video and telephone talk-back, they are just an expensive anachronism.

People who make such remarks completely miss the point of what communication at work is all about. Real communication requires the use of a plurality of methods, not just one or two. Oral communication between managers and staff is clearly the best, but it fails to achieve its full effectiveness if it is not backed up by other means. A well organised notice-board system will not be a futile effort if it is not backed up by a house journal, but it will certainly not be as effective as it could be. Video displays to staff are a worthwhile tool, but they suffer from the fact that, unlike the house journal, the information cannot be absorbed by the employees as and when they individually want it; few organisations are rich enough to give every employee an individual videocassette once a month!

Permutations of communication 'packages' are legion, but all must be tailored to the particular operation, product, person, department, etc. Whatever 'package' an organisation does finally end up with, a house journal is likely to be an important element: each year, the number of house journals being published shows a healthy increase.

One of the main reasons for this may be that people actually *like* house journals — from senior management to front-line workforce, they enjoy the journal, whether it be a single cyclostyled sheet or a glossy brochure, so long as its content has been carefully made to be interesting. This point must be stressed. A boring house journal, containing nothing more than reprints of the company's press releases, simply will not be read — however glossy. A journal containing material that is of interest to employees and which is appropriately presented (depending upon the means of the organisation) can be one of management's most useful tools. This does not mean that you have to try for wall-to-wall colour in every issue — far from it, because all you may be able to afford is a cyclostyled sheet — but it does mean that you must think about what the employees want to read, giving equal weight to the recent financial results and the exploits of departmental football teams.

In smaller organisations house journals are produced by staff members, but larger ones usually employ industrial editors, who may themselves have quite a big staff. The British Association of Industrial Editors, founded in 1949, now has a membership of about 1000. It has been extremely influential in raising standards, through training courses, examinations and its annual Editing for Industry awards. Before the 1950s, however, there were very few full-time, trained journalists producing house journals: the job was almost exclusively done in-house, by people who required some training. So, too, do professional journalists, because the transition from magazines or newspapers to house journals requires the learning of new skills. Often these skills are merely activities which the professional did years ago but has long forgotten — an industrial editor has to know how to do virtually everything involved in the production of the journal — but in other cases genuinely new skills will be required: even the most highly qualified of editors may never have had to think too much about the minutiae of commissioning a photographer, for example. Suitable training courses are run by The Industrial Society and by the British Association of Industrial Editors. A useful book for beginners in the art is *The House Journal Handbook* (revised edition 1987) by Peter C. Jackson, published by The Industrial Society.

Before you decide to take on a house journal, there are a few questions you must consider:

- who are the readers?
- what is the publication going to do?
- what type of publication is it to be?
- how often should it appear?

Who are the readers?

Strangely, many editors who should know better seem to produce publications *just for the sake of the publications*. This may be permissible, even praiseworthy, in the upper reaches of the academic world, where publications are produced for the benefit of a few experts and for posterity, but is not frightfully useful if what an organisation wants is an effective house journal. The first job of the manager is to make sure that the editor of the house journal keeps one thing in mind: concern yourself with the employees who will be receiving the publication and, with luck, reading it.

Before you even start to think about the format or approach of the journal, you or its editor should be trying to compile, as accurately as you can within means that are almost invariably limited, a 'readership profile'. What this slightly frightening phrase means is that you want a breakdown of the journal's readership into various useful categories. The degree to which you and/or the editor can do this varies from company to company — and some editors will know their 'markets' instinctively — but the task should not be too difficult. Shut the office door, take the telephone off the hook, and write down on a sheet of paper as many questions as you can of the following type:

- what percentage of employees are male, what percentage female?
- will the journal be going to ex-employees as well as to employees?

- how many of the readers work overseas?
- is there a broad split between those working in offices and those working on the shop floor(s)?
- are parts of the organisation in widely disparate regions (for example, some in the Southeast and others in Scotland)?
- what kinds of newspapers and magazines do the employees normally read?
- what are the employees' sporting and social interests?
- are some parts of the organisation profitable and others not?

If you have written down all your questions on a single sheet of paper you have not been doing your job properly. The more questions of this type you can pose yourself the better. Of course, you will never be able to find out the answers to all of them — in fact, it might serve to confuse rather than enlighten you if you did. But you should do your best to find out the basics. If possible, you (assuming for the moment you are the editor, either amateur or professional) should visit the various sites where the journal will be read, to meet the people and get the *feel* of the kind of journal they would like to read.

Once all this has been done, don't just throw your 'readership profile' document away. Type it up (or get it typed up) and circulate copies to anyone within the organisation who might have a useful contribution to make — for example, local trade-union representatives. Once you have incorporated any good ideas from other people, make sure you keep the final version in a permanent form — in a file or on a disc. Have a look at it every now and then over the years, as your journal — one hopes! — goes from strength to strength, and ask yourself: 'Am I meeting the information and entertainment needs of these people as I set out to do?'

What is the publication going to do?

Before you start a house journal you should draw up some form of 'policy statement'. The details of this will vary, but the important thing to remember is: have one! The 'policy statement' is a document stating the function of the journal and the chain of responsibility that will allow you and/or the editor to carry out that function. You might even consider forming a committee representing all employee levels and locations just for the purpose of thrashing out these points. Find out from senior management what they want the journal to communicate, and find out from the people on the shop floor what they want the journal to communicate to them. Determine the extent of the editor's freedom of action. Ask people how the journal should treat 'difficult' topics, such as redundancies or strikes. Have it set down in writing whether the editor can use company facilities for printing, photography, writing, design, transport, mailing, and so on, or whether outside suppliers must be laid on. Find out who your readers will be — everyone in the organisation, a section of the organisation, both employees and shareholders, everyone in sight (including possibly the press), or whatever.

Once you have a definitive statement of the journal's policy, have it typed up and get it approved by senior management. That way, if you later run into squalls, you can point to the statement and demonstrate that, if the managing director does not like what the journal is doing, he or she should have thought about it earlier.

What type of publication is it to be?

For many years house journals were either (a) newsletters or (b) magazines, with few if any other options. Then there appeared variety (c), the newspaper, which is probably the commonest type today. However, there has been a good deal of experimentation with hybrids of these three basic types: portmanteau words of varying degrees of vileness, such as 'magapaper' and 'paperzine', have come into existence to describe these.

The simplest form of house journal is the newsletter. At its most rudimentary, it is a single cyclostyled sheet, but some newsletters can comprise a couple of dozen pages, 'typeset' in justified columns using an electronic typewriter or a word processor, printed on the company's offset-litho machine, and bound attractively in a coloured cover. Often newsletters represent management putting their toes in the water before opting for (or not opting for) a full-blooded, well printed house organ, but in fact they are ideal for communicating with smallish numbers of people — up to about 500 — where the costs of producing a magazine or newspaper would be prohibitive. A further use of newsletters is as supplements to more sophisticated house journals: for example, a glossy magazine for general consumption might live alongside a crudely produced newsletter designed for managers only.

Never underestimate the power of even the most primitively produced newsletter. In many ways, the fact that the newsletter is such a rudimentary means of communication can actually help it, because the staff feel that its very simplicity means that they have a closer bond with management. One medium-sized publishing company has for years produced a weekly duplicated and indifferently typed sheet. When management suggested something more glamorous the staff objected strongly — they liked it the way it was. Pertinently, they also pointed out that they would rather the money were spent on pay rises!

Newspapers were not widely used as house journals until quite recently, but their popularity has been growing — especially since the introduction of the web offset-litho printing process (which allows realistically priced print-runs of only a few thousand copies) and the availability of full-colour printing on newsprint. Both of these developments helped cause a revolution in communication with employees. Newspapers are now used in larger organisations, where the circulation — for example, in a nationalised industry — can be as high as half a million. They usually carry mainly news stories and relevant photographs, with some features. Normally they are tabloids — that is, they are the same shape as newspapers such as the *Daily Mail*.

Despite the recent growth in popularity of the newspaper as a house journal, magazines are still widely used. The approach used varies broadly, from the fireside chat to the technical abstract — as does the circulation, which may be anything from a few hundred to many thousands. Likewise, these magazines may use only a single colour or be in full colour, and their sizes, extents and paper qualities differ vastly. Their basic use, as in most commercial magazines, is to carry features and photographs, plus a small number of news items. One reason why magazines are so popular as house journals is probably that their production gives huge scope for creativity on the part of the editor and the designer.

A halfway house between the newspaper and the magazine is the news magazine, which normally has a format, editorial style and production quality rather like that of *Time* or *Time Out* — that is, it carries both news items and short features, it has relatively little colour, the style is more formal than that of a newspaper, and it is printed on thinner paper than the conventional magazine.

Aside from these main types of house journal, there are many variations. Look through a couple of dozen journals and you will certainly find a few. However, if you are planning to launch a house journal, it seems sensible to opt for one of the tried and tested types rather than a designer's or editor's brainwave. Above all, do not try to mix the various formats: tabloid treatment in a magazine environment will be just as unacceptable to employees as fact-packed copy dressed up to be a tabloid. Readers of the house journal will be happy only if they find the type of material they expect in the usual medium that it appears in. This may be an idea that is intellectually repugnant to you, but remember the fate of the *News on Sunday*.

How often should it appear?

The most important question to ask in terms of frequency of publication is: what kind of information are we trying to get across? General features on production and export will keep for months; news of retirements, appointments, promotions and wage deals may have already been communicated by other means. There are in fact two possible roles a house journal can have. It can be a journal of record or a conveyor of news. Both roles are equally valid, and the best house journals perform both — recording the big news which everyone already knows (and, usefully, quite possibly correcting misunderstandings that may have arisen if that news was conveyed through the grapevine, over a Tannoy system, etc.) and conveying the less significant news.

If you want to go for real instant journalism, you can opt for daily publication. There are a lot of problems, though. First, in a large organisation, it is difficult actually to distribute the journal to everyone on the day of publication. Second, and more important, with this frequency, all you can hope to produce is something pretty tatty in terms of both content and presentation, and so it is doubtful whether such a hastily thrown-together document will really communicate very much.

Weekly newspapers are an option only if you are prepared to pay for a special department to produce them, although a weekly or fortnightly duplicated newsletter is more feasible, especially in organisations with only a few tens or hundreds of employees.

Most house journals, whatever their form, are monthlies — or more-or-less monthlies. Some companies publish thirteen times a year, so that the journal comes out every four weeks, while others publish on v ten or eleven times a year, missing out during summer and/or winter holiday breaks. If your company cannot manage monthly publication, you might think about producing the journal every six weeks — although this means that contributors and letter-writers can never quite remember when the journal is supposed to be coming out, and so have to be chased for their copy at the eleventh hour.

Probably a better option is bi-monthly publication. Of course, a bi-monthly journal cannot be expected to contain much by way of news — if news takes two months to percolate through your organisation then there is something seriously wrong with your other communication systems — but, well produced and containing a modicum of news amidst a plethora of informative features, it can be a useful communication tool. The same comments apply to quarterly journals, of course.

One option worth thinking about is a combination of frequencies — for example, a weekly duplicated newspaper complemented by a quarterly glossy magazine. However, whatever frequency or combination of frequencies you decide on, publish *regularly* rather than just when the whim takes you: not only do the employees and the accounts department prefer it, typesetters and printers are usually too busy to take on work at the drop of a hat.

Other considerations

When considering any form of report to employees you should spend a fair deal of your energy in getting the tone right. The majority of your audience will probably be unfamiliar with accounting terminology, strategic market thinking and the like, and it may even be that some of your readers are of limited educational ability and therefore unused to absorbing complex information through the medium of the written word. There is thus a temptation to talk down to the readers: avoid it all costs. People know when they are being talked down to and they invariably resent it.

Conversely, it is vital that you keep the language (and the diagrams) simple, because people are much more likely to read — and understand on first reading — articles which use short sentences and short words. This applies throughout the organisation. No one feels insulted by simple language. What they may feel insulted by is a truly banal message. If you would feel embarrassed reading the report to a friend, then the tone is wrong: you are patronising your readers.

The format of the report is another important consideration. The best advice is: change it only if you feel you really need to. If you are constantly chopping and changing, your audience will see each new format as just 'Their' flavour of the month. People generally prefer consistency, as you will realise as soon as you think about how many commercial newspapers and magazines — *Reader's Digest*, to take a random example — have successfully stuck to essentially the same format for not just years but often decades. Of course, you may want to modify the format a little from time to time, but introduce changes gradually.

Formats of annual employee reports have to strike a happy balance. If the reports are too cheaply produced people are likely to think that they are no more than a token gesture, that management really does not care about them, or that the organisation must be in a bad way. Conversely, over-lavish reports can be regarded as a 'con job', and will surely arouse resentment if, for example, the workers have just been told that they cannot have a pay rise.

When you are producing an annual employee report, rather than a house journal, one important element will be the chairman's (or chairwoman's) message. (If the chairperson is non-executive, then he or she is the wrong person to write this report: the chief executive should do it.) If the chairman's message is a long, formal statement, then it is unlikely to be read. Otherwise, though, people are interested in the chief executive's impressions of how the organisation is doing, the challenges it faces, and the general details of planned future strategies. People may disagree with those strategies, but they are much less likely to become disaffected if they understand the reasons behind them.

The chairman's statement should, in essence, be a summary of the annual employee report — it does not matter if the information is repeated elsewhere in more detail, because quite often people will read only the chairman's statement, and those who read the entire report will find the broad overview of assistance when they come to look at the detailed picture. The chairman's message should be kept reasonably short — certainly under 1500 words — and if it is over 200 words it should probably be broken up using snappy subheadings (although beware overusing these). One thing the chief executive should be sure to do in the message is to *thank* the workers. People do appreciate their contributions to the organisation being recognised and acknowledged, and they most certainly notice if they are not.

Larger organisations often use audiovisual means — almost always video — to back up the printed report. This has many advantages. For example, when people are gathered together to watch a video, they can ask questions about or discuss its content, so that misunderstandings can be cleared up. Also, you can be sure that people have watched the video, whereas they may treat their copy of the printed report as just so much junk mail. But video alone is useless without the printed version, because people forget much of what they have seen and have no means of referring back. And, of course, making videos is an expensive business, almost certainly requiring the use of specialist outside staff.

Professional outsiders for printed media are much less expensive, and often you will find that they can do a better job than anyone within the firm; it is, after all, not much of a saving if you lose thousands of pounds through poor staff relations which could have been improved if you had spent a few hundred pounds on a professional editor. The cheapest way of going about this is to have the people within the organisation throw together all the elements of the report or journal, and then to hire a freelance journalist to knock it into shape. Likewise, you will probably have to find an outside designer/illustrator to produce the graphic material and to lay out the pages attractively.

Whatever sort of house journal or annual report you produce, and however you go about it, remember the point of the whole exercise: to communicate. If you fail to communicate then you might just as well save the money.

7 FACE TO FACE

We spend much of our lives speaking to other people, but something strange happens to many of us when we are asked to speak in front of a group or in a formalised situation. For reasons which are less than rational, it is an activity many of us like to get out of if we can.

However, increasingly we are called upon to make presentations to groups — some small, others large — in a variety of situations, and we are often judged by our performance on these occasions. The curious thing is that good communicative managers positively enjoy such encounters; and, even if they cannot totally smother the fear that they may make a fool of themselves, recognise that the face-to-face encounter can contribute a lot to communication within the organisation and to good relations with employees.

In this chapter we shall look briefly at a few tips on how to speak more effectively to a group, how to hold better meetings, and how to conduct better interviews.

Preparing to speak

To fail to prepare is, basically, to prepare to fail.

The first thing to do is to prepare yourself by asking yourself a few pointed questions.

- Why are you giving the talk? Get straight in your mind your precise objectives. Are you planning to sell a product or idea, or to instruct, or what? Try to write down a one-sentence summary of your objectives.
- Who are you going to be addressing? How many of them are there going to be, why are they there, and what kind of people are they? If you do not sort this out, much of your audience will spend their whole time wondering if they have come to the wrong room.

- Where are you going to be speaking? Ideally, choose the venue to suit yourself and the audience but, if you cannot do that, at least go and have a look at it beforehand — and preferably practice speaking in it. If possible, have the seating rearranged the way you want it. Find out where things like the light switches are, and try to reduce any possibilities of your audience being distracted by outside influences. If the room looks out onto a nudist colony, for example, it might be best to learn how to draw the blinds.
- When will the talk be given, and how long should it last? Try never to give a talk immediately after lunch because people are likely to be feeling sleepy, especially if they have a few drinks inside them. Also, see if you can select a time of day that suits your own body clock. Never go on too long. The best way of ensuring that you do not is to time your speech beforehand, and then add 25 per cent. During the talk itself, keep an eye on the time. Bear in mind that people usually concentrate well for the first twenty minutes, and then their attention begins to wander.

The other aspect of preparation is that of the material itself. Unstructured, rambling talks are usually hard for the audience to concentrate on. Unless the main points are made absolutely explicit the audience will probably soon forget them. So you want to make sure that, not only does your talk say all you want it to say, it *conveys* all you want it to convey. The way to do this is to prepare your subject matter carefully to ensure that your talk is both structured and lively.

The way to start is to use the system of notes we discussed in connection with report writing (see page 67). Once you have recorded all your immediate ideas, it is a good idea to put them to one side for a while. When you return to your notes you may have thought of other ideas to add. If the logical ordering of ideas was not immediately self-evident when you were brainstorming your notes, it probably will have become so by now. Also, you will probably find that you have more ideas than you can possibly cram into the allotted space of time, so prune ruthlessly anything that is not strictly relevant.

Now is the time to concentrate on, not the beginning, but the middle of the talk. Bearing in mind all the constraints of time, work out first what you *must* tell the audience, and make sure that all such topics are covered. Then include as much as possible of what you *should* tell the audience, and finally, if there is still time, include extra things that may be helpful to them — including jokes, if they really are funny, because good jokes prolong people's attention spans.

The overall structure of your talk should be as in writing a report (see page 69). First tell them what you are going to tell them, then tell them, and finally tell them what you have told them. More formally, a good structure is this:

- State the proposition.
- Anticipate objections by stating them yourself, and then saying why they are invalid.
- Prove your case, selecting the very best reasons for your proposition. Giving too many reasons will befog your main thrust — and anyway you can always come out with your other reasons during question time.
- Show your practical evidence, using examples of the facts you are relying on. Do not slant the evidence in any way, because if you try to do so you will inevitably be caught out.
- Conclude by repeating the proposition.

The use of down-to-earth examples is important, because they keep the audience interested and make what you are saying more relevant to them. For instance, one astronomer has a habit, when talking about gaseous nebulae, of pointing out that some of them contain enough ethyl alcohol to fill a hollowed-out Earth with neat whisky. This is a much more effective way of conveying the information to the audience than giving the figure in cubic miles, and certainly ensures that everyone suddenly becomes interested in gaseous nebulae. Using such analogies is particularly vital if your subject matter is basically boring — which, by the nature of things, sometimes it will have to be.

The opening of your talk is important. Ideally, you want to grab the interest of your audience immediately, so try to find something arresting: 'Unaccustomed as I am to public speaking' is not recommended. One frequent speaker often starts his talks with: 'Jeez, I'm terrified.' This not only wakens the audience, because it is so unconventional, it makes sure that for at least the next few minutes they are on his side, so that they pay attention and clap in all the right places. Of course, such an option is not open to you on all occasions, but certainly you should seek out some attention-grabbing one-liner.

Immediately after the one-liner, tell the audience why it is important that they listen to what you say, and then give a brief resumé of your subject matter — in other words, tell them what you are going to tell them. You may also wish to explain the objective of the talk; if not, you should be sure that it is obvious throughout the whole of the time you are speaking.

The concluding section of your talk should be just that: conclusive. Allowing it to peter out with a muttered 'I think that's all I've got to say' is a big mistake. Remember that your final words are the ones that are most likely to stick in the heads of your audience, so reiterate your main points as clearly, as briefly and as vividly as you can.

It is helpful, in this context, if you write out in full your closing — and indeed your opening — sentences and have them in front of you as you speak. Apart from that, however, your notes should be as brief as possible, and consist solely of keywords written on cards. It may very well be that you have written your talk out in full, but even so you should reduce it to keywords. People want you to speak to them, not to read to them. If you find the thought of speaking in such an *ex tempore* fashion too terrifying, write the keywords in coloured ink in the margins of the typed-up version of your speech, and resort to reading only on those few occasions when you have to. If you really do have to read your speech — and one of the best public speakers in favour of CND always reads his — then apologise to your audience at the outset. If you admit it as a failing, at least you will have the audience on your side. But the best thing is usually to work from keywords written NICE AND BIG on a handful of cards.

Nerves

Surveys have shown that fear of giving a public speech is one of the top ten fundamental human terrors — up there with fear of heights! So if the idea strikes panic in your heart, be reassured by one thing: you are not alone. For some unknown reason, people are much more frightened of speaking to an audience of twenty than they are of appearing on radio or television before an audience of millions.

Pre-speech nerves will never leave you, and probably they shouldn't. Nervousness flushes your body with adrenalin, producing what psychologists call the 'flight or fight response'.

You can use the adrenalin to 'fight' — in other words, to give a dynamic, thrusting talk. If you are unable to do this, be comforted by the fact that, however nervous and shaky you are on the inside, the audience hardly ever notices.

Quivering voices and hands or worried frowns will of course be spotted, so do your best to find some way of calming your nerves before you start. Thorough preparation is one of the best ways, because it gives you a lot of confidence to know that you are in full mastery of your subject. A small drink immediately beforehand may help you relax, but don't overdo it! Thinking about something totally unrelated during the ten or so minutes before you start is a good way of reducing your nervousness: why not chat to someone about the cricket scores? You can try deep breathing or neck exercises — both of which can help relax you.

Best of all, however, are two very simple things:

- don't worry about yourself
- remember that the audience are probably quite nice people really

Putting yourself across

Curiously, although our basic communicatory medium is words, words themselves make an extremely small contribution to the total message when we are speaking to people. Research has shown that the contribution of the words is as low as 7 per cent, while the tone of voice contributes 38 per cent and body language a staggering 55 per cent.

However small their contribution, the words are fundamentally important: imagine trying to make a speech without them! The key to good speech-making is to use simple, direct language, avoiding jargon wherever possible. Talk in sentences, just as you would write: if you string everything together with 'ands' and 'buts' people will have difficulty following you and will soon lose interest. Remember to talk in terms of concrete things, not abstractions, and, as we saw above, do not worry about being too liberal with practical examples.

Once you have the right words, the way in which you say them becomes crucial. We know from everyday experience how an apparently innocent sentence can be transformed into a deadly insult if spoken sarcastically. Of course, the modulations of your vocal expression when giving a talk should be more subtle than sarcasm, but the principle is much the same. If you say something enthusiastically (even if you are only acting it) then your audience is likely to emulate your perceived enthusiasm. If you stress some sentences more than others, you can help get across your main points. If you vary your speed of delivery and the pitch of your voice you will hold the audience's attention much better than if you deliver your spiel in a dull monotone. Pause for a little while after you have made one of your main points: it gives time for the point to sink in. Speak clearly and loudly, because people will soon become bored if they have to strain to work out what you are saying. And, finally, do not be afraid to ham it up if you are speaking to a large group. Stage actors ham much more than, say, television ones because otherwise they fail to communicate emotions throughout a large auditorium. If you are addressing several hundred people, you have to think of yourself as being essentially a stage actor, and it is virtually impossible for you to ham it up too much.

You have the right words and you have worked out the various ways of saying them. Lastly you must consider your use of body language.

We have all slept through lectures where the speaker has adopted a glassy-eyed look, gone pale, and stared over the audience's heads. You should stand square-on to the audience and look at them, letting your gaze rove so that you make frequent eye contact with everyone there. Try not to stand behind something like a desk or a lectern and thereby create a barrier between yourself and your audience. Particularly if you are nervous, force yourself not to use distracting mannerisms, such as waving your hands around all over the place or jingling the keys in your pocket.

Overall, the art of good body language is to be natural. This, you might say, is easier said than done but, if you concentrate on getting the message across and stop worrying about yourself, you will have every chance of coming over naturally.

We cannot leave the subject of putting yourself across without a few words on visual aids. These can be useful to break up long talks, to convey information that might be difficult to put over in speech, and to give the audience something else to do rather than just sit there and listen.

Be adventurous with visual aids, but do not overdo them. You should carefully plan how they will fit in with your talk, but do not rely on them entirely — because, if you do, the equipment will inevitably break down (obviously, always check the equipment a few minutes before you start). Visuals should be large, simple and graphic — a bar chart rather than a column of figures, for example — and you should not try to force too much visual information at people too quickly. If using slides, give the audience time to look at them, but do not leave the slide still showing while you move on to a new topic: looking at one thing and listening to another is confusing. A final point is that, when using visual aids, you should remember to talk to the audience, not to the screen.

What is a meeting?

The snappy reply is that most of them are a waste of time. Many vitally important decisions in industry are made at meetings, and yet meetings themselves tend to be unproductive, expensive and just plain boring.

One reason for this is that there are often too many people present, so that inevitably much of the time is wasted discussing irrelevances. In any organisation it is very likely that better decisions would be reached in half the time if there were only half as many people there. Also, a strong, well organised chair can suppress the trivia, elicit the important information from the people best acquainted with it, and immeasurably speed up decision making.

A great danger is that meetings can become an end in themselves — something especially true of regular meetings, which often take place just because they always have done. In one small company of about ten people there has been for years, in addition to other meetings, a regularly weekly meeting which has to be attended by six people. Frequently this meeting goes on all day. Most of the business could be covered in about an hour but, because the meeting has traditionally been long and boring, sheer management inertia means that it remains so.

Responsibilities of the meeting leader

Meetings differ widely in their size, composition, organisation and purpose. It is fundamental to the success of any meeting that the purpose is clear and relevant: if not, the meeting not only wastes valuable time and effort, it can cause frustration and misunderstanding and generally demotivate people. The purposes of meetings may differ, but broadly speaking they are concerned with one or more of the following: information giving, information gathering, persuading, problem solving, and decision taking. The way meetings are organised and the roles of their leaders vary enormously.

The leader's responsibilities include:

- defining the meeting's purpose
- planning and preparation
- attending regularly (assuming it is a regular meeting)
- conducting the meeting efficiently
- controlling the discussion (but not doing all the talking!)
- dealing effectively with problem situations and individuals
- ensuring the meeting keeps to time
- making sure everyone participates
- making sure the purpose of the meeting is achieved, and that members know what is expected of them as a result
- liaising with the secretary (especially if a record of the meeting is required)

This is not the place to go into all the details of such matters as planning and preparation for meetings. Instead we shall look at the aspects most important in terms of communication: chairing a meeting, stating your case at a meeting, and following up.

The skills of chairing meetings — four useful tools

The leader of a meeting has a number of available tools to help maintain control of the discussion. The four main ones are processing of the discussion, statements, questions, and summaries.

Processing the discussion really means imposing a structure on the meeting. The structure is by no means a complex one: rather like a good story, a good meeting must have a beginning, a middle and an end.

At the start, the leader should be ready to welcome the members and should open the meeting in a friendly manner, thus helping to create the right climate. Maintaining this climate depends on the leader's ability to inspire confidence and command respect.

This can be achieved by demonstrating that you consider the meeting important, that you have planned and prepared for it, and that you know how to run it — although you need some flexibility, since you may have to adapt your plan to suit the needs of the members

The meeting should formally open with an introductory statement summarising what the meeting is for, what is known, what is required, and how it is going to be tackled. Thereafter the degree of your participation will vary according to the type of meeting, but you should remember that, the greater your participation, the less the participation of the members. Or, to put it more simply: don't talk too much.

One problem that can arise, especially in discussions of emotive subjects where people hold strong views, is the matter of separating out the facts from the opinions expressed as facts. One approach that can be helpful is a sort of five-part plan. First, solicit information: ask members for exactly this and keep them to the point. Second, reach a clear picture based on the facts and on summarising (see below). Third, seek opinions from the members. Fourth, evaluate fact and opinion together. Fifth, and last, decide where you should go from here.

Throughout, you should be aware of the needs of the group, drawing out the quiet members and controlling the garrulous ones. Certainly you should prevent the situation where small splinter groups of members start having private debates.

After the main body of the meeting is over, you have to bring it to an end. You should make a final summary confirming the conclusions of the meeting, stressing the action that is to be taken and who is going to take it. The whole purpose of any meeting is achievement of the objective. You need to establish and emphasise this achievement — even if it has not been fully satisfactory — and commend individual and group contributions.

There are three types of statements that you need to make during a meeting, each of which has a different purpose. The opening statement, as we have seen, is necessary to clarify the purpose and objectives of the meeting and define the terms and scope of the discussion. The other two types are statements that you can feed in when necessary to provide information, and those that provide clarification in order to obviate possible misunderstandings.

There are, too, various types of questions you should ask group members in order to maximise participation. There are your *opening* questions, which you should use to point the meeting in the right direction. These should be thought-provoking, should engage the attention of the whole group, and must never be the sort of question that attracts a 'yes' or 'no' answer. Then there are *overhead questions* issued during the meeting. These are addressed to the group as a whole, and are almost certain to elicit some form of useful reply. One specific use of them is to guide the discussion back to the main subject if it has strayed. *Direct questions,* addressed to specific group members, have a number of obvious uses other than simply getting information; also useful are *redirected questions,* whereby you pass a question raised by one group member directly across to another. Similarly, a question raised by one person can be relayed to the group as a whole for discussion. Finally, there is the *reverse question,* where you ask the person posing the question to try to answer it themselves: 'I was about to ask you the same question. What do you think?'

The fourth major tool at your disposal is the summary — not just your final summary of the meeting, but also interim ones to indicate progress or its lack, refocus the discussion, tie up one point so that you can advance the discussion to the next, highlight important points, guide the person who is taking the minutes, and clarify misunderstandings. Your final summary should establish the group's conclusions, state what actions should be taken, and give the members a sense of what has been achieved.

Both interim and final summaries should be put to members for their agreement. This also helps the minute taker and cuts down on unnecessary later argument over the minutes' accuracy.

Stating your case at a meeting

However well people have prepared and planned for a meeting, it can all be wasted if they do not state their case coherently. Some people find it particularly difficult to put over their ideas to a group, and will remain silent for fear of ridicule.

Effective speakers know exactly what they want to say. They know how they are going to present their argument. By contrast, ineffective speakers are those who are not clear in their own minds about what they want to say, nor about how they want to say it. They dart about in a confusion of verbiage, following no set plan and developing no logical argument. In other words, they waffle.

Here are a few ways which can help you solve such problems:

- Be sure of the facts. Sum them up briefly, defining any unfamiliar terms. State your proposition.
- Face the snags — do not attempt to hide them. Weigh what is against you, and anticipate objections. (This also helps you evaluate the soundness of your own reasoning beforehand.)
- Prove your case, selecting and highlighting the best reasons in your favour. It is the quality, not the quantity, of your reasons that is important.
- Show practical evidence, having relevant examples at your fingertips. But do be careful not to slant the evidence: it does not work.
- Conclude your statement by repeating the proposition.

Minutes

Minutes are an essential, although their nature will vary depending upon the type of meeting. Formal committees sometimes require detailed minutes, whereas informal meetings really require no more than a list of things that are to be done. Whatever the case, the important things about the minutes are that they should be produced quickly and accurately and should show what action is required and by whom.

If you are leading a meeting, there are several ways in which you can help the minute taker. As noted above, you should give interim summaries at the end of the discussion of each point on the agenda. Spend a few minutes with the minute taker beforehand, outlining your general plan of the meeting (this is invaluable to the minute taker) and explaining any unfamiliar terms that may be used. Also, the minute taker should be encouraged to interrupt during the meeting if he or she does not fully understand something. Otherwise the minutes are likely to be a nonsense — and it will not be the minute taker's fault: it will be yours.

Where actions have to be taken, deadlines should be discussed during the meeting and recorded in the minutes, so that it is easier for you to monitor later progress. These should be firm deadlines, not vague ones. Phrases like 'as soon as possible' mean different things to different people.

Interviewing

An interview can be regarded as a type of meeting involving only two people, one of whom is in the driving seat. When you are interviewing someone you are conducting a type of conversation, but with a purpose. You are responsible for controlling the conversation and achieving the purpose.

There are any number of reasons for conducting interviews — selection, counselling, discussion of grievances, discipline, appraisal or termination. Here we shall look only at the general skills required. For more detailed discussion of the different types of interview, see my book *The Action-centred Leader.*

If you are to conduct an interview, it is essential that you know its objective. You cannot control and plan it unless you know exactly what you are aiming for; nor can you be certain afterwards that you have achieved your objective if you were not certain what it was in the first place.

Once you know your objective, you can start preparing for the interview. Obviously, there are some circumstances in which it is very difficult to plan ahead — for example, when someone drops in unexpectedly to discuss a problem. However, usually you should have prepared yourself in advance in three main areas. The first of these is your own mental preparation, deciding how long the interview should last and what approach you should adopt, bearing in mind both the objective and your knowledge of what type of person the interviewee is. Second comes environmental preparation — the room you are going to use, the seating arrangements, and so on, right down to the provision of ashtrays. And the final area of preparation is in terms of the material you will require — personal files, application forms, relevant statistics, copies of the company rules, and so forth.

All the preparation in the world will be of little use to you if you fail to develop your own conversational skills in order to control the progress of the discussion, make sure there is common understanding, and elicit the necessary information.

As when you are leading a meeting, asking the right questions is the key to getting the right answers. Think before you phrase a question, and ask yourself what you want that question to do. If you want to encourage the interviewee to expand, do more talking, and convey to you not just information but feelings and attitudes (that is, subjective as well as objective information), then use *open questions,* ones which cannot be answered by a simple 'yes' or 'no'. A question like 'How are you enjoying your job?' can produce an immensely informative response — as well as giving the interviewee confidence. The *closed question,* the one that requires a 'yes' or a 'no', likewise has its uses. It can bring the conversation back to the point if it has strayed, and it summarises the discussion so far. It helps you tie up one point so that you can move on to the next, and to make sure that both yourself and the interviewee share a common understanding. It can be used also to shut up garrulous interviewees, but the most dedicated wafflers will carry on regardless. Such people are best treated to a barrage of *specific questions,* questions to which the only possible response is a specific datum: 'When did you start work here?' Of course, this is also the type of question to use if you really do want some hard answers. If, on the other hand, you want to keep the interviewee talking, use the *reverse question,* which we discussed above in the context of meetings. The one type of question to be careful about is the *leading question.* 'Don't you think it's disgusting that the company has moved over to flexitime?' is a way of encouraging the interviewee to agree with you, the boss, even if he or she in fact thinks flexitime is a great idea. Your net information gain from a 'yes' answer is zero, because you do not know if the interviewee really agrees with you or is simply trying to keep you happy. However, if skilfully used, leading questions can be helpful. They can enable you to find out, for example, if the interviewee has the strength of character to disagree with you, and the intellectual acuity to justify the disagreement. Also, they can draw out shy interviewees in the initial stages of the interview. Finally, there is the *hypothetical question,* the 'what if?' type of question, which is excellent as a means of testing the abilities of interviewees and thus is especially useful in selection interviews. 'If we were to offer you the job, how would you restructure the department?' is a question that can — and should — tell you a very great deal.

A good interviewer alternates between the various types of questions to develop the right style of interview for the particular objective, interviewee and indeed interviewer. Most often, you need to discover not just facts but also feelings and attitudes, so the questions you use will most likely be a combination of open, closed and specific ones.

Listening to the answers is as important as phrasing the questions correctly — especially since the answer to one question is likely to determine the shape of the next. You might feel that the interviewee has failed to supply enough information, or that there is something a bit rum about the answer, and so wish to pursue the point a little further. Some people can follow their instincts on this, but most of us have to concentrate on listening very carefully — listening to the words used and the way in which they are spoken, and looking for any body-language clues that might help us. Another thing we have to listen for is what is *not* being said.

You should not only listen, you should be seen to be listening. This is an important part of establishing and maintaining rapport with the interviewee, and encouraging him or her to speak freely. Eye contact is the major way in which we show that we are listening. If we spend less than 30 per cent of the time making eye contact the interviewee feels that we are not really interested, but if we spend more than 60 per cent of the time in eye contact we are likely to give the interviewee the impression that we are aggressive. In fact, most of us get the right balance naturally in our everyday conversations: the trouble is that, during an interview, both people are just a little bit nervous and so tend to react unnaturally.

As in meetings, statements and summaries are useful tools, and for exactly the same reasons, but the most important thing you have to do in an interview is to develop rapport with the interviewee. The skills we have been discussing will all help in this, but something more is required. You should become interested in the other person — develop empathy. Try to understand their feelings, so that you too become involved in the discussion and communicate more clearly. There really is no substitute for genuine interest and concern on your part: if you yawn occasionally, or keep glancing at your watch, you are telling the interviewee that you are not interested, and the message will be clearly understood — and, quite justifiably, bitterly resented.

At a more technical level, you can assist rapport by being aware of a few simple procedures. Assure the interviewee that you are in control of the interview by directing its course throughout: this gives the person the confidence that the interview will actually achieve something. Make sure that the purpose of the interview is quite clearly stated, and give initial guidance as to how the interview will proceed towards that goal: this gives interviewees confidence because they are reassured that the two of you are not likely to be talking at cross-purposes. Nevertheless, although you have given the interviewee the message that you are in control, do not monopolise the session. Encourage the person to talk freely and to relax, using encouraging nods, smiles and comments. Allow the person the maximum possible freedom within the framework which you have established of a well controlled interview.

Interviewing, conducting meetings and giving talks are all activities usually concerned with communication inside an organisation. Taken together, they are obviously hugely important. However, communication from within the organisation to the outside world is equally important, and we shall tackle this topic in the next chapter.

8 COMMUNICATING WITH THE OUTSIDE WORLD

There are three principal ways in which we communicate with people outside our organisation: through meetings, through letters, and through telephone conversations. Of these, meetings tend to happen only from time to time, but we are likely to be in daily contact with the outside world through letters and telephone conversations. We have already discussed, in the preceding chapter, the basic art of the meeting, which is little affected by whether the members are from within the organisation or from outside it, so in this chapter we shall concentrate on the other two ways.

About 25 per cent of your time is likely to be spent in writing and dictating, and most of this 25 per cent is likely to be taken up by correspondence. Many people in business are reluctant to write letters, preferring to use the telephone or some other method of communication. However, some letters are essential. The written word can provide a permanent record and an opportunity for the recipient to read the message several times over to understand it and its implications fully. Moreover, complex ideas are often better communicated in print: the subject matter can be better prepared and the words more carefully chosen so that the precise meaning you want to convey really is conveyed.

Some of us try to avoid business writing. This is often because the writer is aware of his or her own possible limitations in terms of writing fluency. Such a situation often results in the worst excrescences of 'officialese' or 'technobabble'. In reality, the best way of approaching letter writing is to use simple words and simple sentences: write it the way you would say it. If you do this, there is a good chance the recipient will comprehend your message on first reading, and you will reduce the chances of later arguments because of misunderstandings.

How important are business letters? The answer is: very. Often they will be received as part of a fistful of other business letters, and so, if they are badly written or offputting in general presentation, they will be put at the bottom of the pile — where they may well stay in perpetuity. Moreover, your business letter is a sort of ambassador for your organisation: if it is badly put together it will put not only yourself but also your entire company in an unfavourable light, which could mean that you are throwing away a lot of potential business.

An aspect of letter writing not considered here is the matter of working effectively with your secretary. We shall discuss this topic in the next chapter.

The other daily channel of communication to the outside world is, of course, the telephone. Most of us frequently use the telephone at work, either to respond to people's enquiries or to obtain information from them. Very often it is the only point of contact we have with our customers. How you treat your callers will, just as with the letters you write, reflect upon your organisation. Most of us would agree that we want to create an image of ourselves and our organisations which embodies helpfulness, efficiency and friendliness. Aims are one thing; results are all too frequently another. Here are a few of the ways in which managers often give outsiders an extremely unfavourable view of their organisations:

- failing to return calls
- not answering promptly
- eating, drinking or smoking while on the telephone — all can be heard only too clearly at the other end
- leaving people hanging on without periodically reassuring them that you are trying to deal with their query
- refusing to give your own name — a particular crime of the civil service
- holding two conversations at once
- asking the caller to ring back later (especially if, when they call back at the requested time, you are out)
- transferring people hither and thither through the organisation
- giving an unintelligible greeting or just saying 'hello' when you pick up the telephone
- a negative attitude
- sounding uncertain about what you are saying
- being evasive, petulant or even rude — much easier over the telephone than when you are speaking with someone face to face
- letting the irritation show in your voice that the telephone went

just as you were in the middle of adding up a column of figures, or at some other inconvenient moment

However much you might regard the telephone as an intrusive distraction, it is vital for the continuing prosperity of your organisation that you use it effectively. No less than 80 per cent of new business is initiated over the telephone, so can you afford to leave your telephone effectiveness to chance?

Preparing to write a letter

The first stage of any writing you do is to prepare yourself.

The initial question you must ask is: What is the purpose of this letter? It may help you if you write down this purpose in a single sentence before you go any further. This will decide the letter's style and tone, and in some cases may show you that it really ought to be written by someone else.

Then you must ask yourself a series of questions about the recipient. Who are you writing to, and how much do they already know about the subject? Do they have any preconceived or strong views on the subject? Are they the person to whom you should be writing? When will the letter be received? And what does the recipient want from the letter?

Physical preparation for letter writing is a far from complex business. First you must collect all the relevant facts and material together. Read any previous correspondence carefully so that you have a clear picture of the current 'state of play'. If you need to refer to a specific file or ledger, do so now rather than when you are in the middle of writing the letter. Once you have your facts assembled, sift through them to select only the ones that are relevant to your message and to the needs of the reader. Finally, make a plan: using a fresh sheet of paper, sort your facts into a logical order. Start with the main burden of the letter and finish by pointing the way ahead — that is, by stating who is to do what next.

Structure and style

Almost all business letters can be written according to a very simple structure:
● introduction

- facts
- action to be taken
- concluding remarks

The introduction to the letter should tell the reader why you are writing it. If the person is someone you know well, of course, you may wish to preface the introduction proper by a few friendly remarks: 'It was good to see you last Thursday to talk about the pollution problem' or something like that. However, keep such remarks to a minimum: without being brusque, you want to get to the point as early as possible. It is often helpful to give the letter a title, for example:

Dear Polly
Invoice number 745
Thank you for your letter of the 8th telling me that ...

Notice the way the letter starts. Today's business language is simple, direct and clear. Expressions like 'we are in receipt of your communication of the 8th inst' and 'with reference to your esteemed enquiry' are relics of the past, and if you use them your reader will immediately assume that you, and your organisation, are stuffy and incompetent.

The next section of the letter consists of your statement of the relevant facts. These you have already sorted out into a logical order, so usually it is easy enough simply to write them out — making sure that they are accurate and complete. However, if there are a lot of facts involved, or if they are very complicated, it may be a good idea to give each new paragraph a heading of its own. If it will make things simpler for the reader, number the paragraphs.

After the facts have been set out, the next task is to state what action is to be taken, and by whom. This is vital, as otherwise all sorts of misunderstanding and confusion can arise. If you are the person who is going to take the action, it is just as important to tell the reader what you are going to do as it is to request that he or she take some particular action, if things are the other way around.

It might seem that your concluding remarks — a polite expression of good will — should be the easiest part to write of the entire letter, but in fact this is very often not the case. You do not want to sound too distant, and yet you do not want to appear too fawningly over-friendly. You might find it useful to make a mental picture of your reader, and to imagine that you are explaining the facts in person.

As we saw above, modern business letter writing is direct and clear, rather than flowery and pompous. In fact, there are many different schools of thought on what is the 'correct' style of letter writing. Some companies even have a house style to which all employees must conform. However, the most important rule for any business writing is that its purpose is to communicate effectively with the reader. If you make that your primary aim, then it really does not matter which style of writing you choose, especially if you remember the three cardinal principles of accuracy, brevity and clarity. We shall look at each of these three in turn.

Accuracy

Make sure that you are saying what you think you are saying: if you are not, you may be (a) making yourself look a fool, (b) running the risk of inadvertently upsetting your reader, (c) creating confusion, or (d) all three. Make sure that you know what the words you are using actually mean (and that you — or at least your secretary! — can spell them), and use them correctly and in the correct context. Do not rely too heavily on your dictionary. It can be a great help with the spelling or meaning of an unfamiliar term, but using it indiscriminately in order to pad your letter or to try to impress the reader inevitably leads to bad, bloated writing and increases the risk of misunderstanding. Another problem with dictionaries is that they are, for obvious reasons, always out of date (although this is less true today, thanks to the use of computers in dictionary compilation). The use of words changes more swiftly than any dictionary can hope to keep up with, so that the meaning of a word 'collected' by the compilers as little as a few years ago may have changed quite radically. For example, only a couple of decades ago you might have used the word 'gay' without a second thought; now you have to have that second thought, and make sure that it is clear from the context what you are saying.

To assist the accuracy of your reader's understanding of your letter, try to use concrete rather than abstract nouns, so that your reader can picture as clearly as possible what you mean. If you find you have to use abstract nouns, be careful to explain clearly what you mean by them.

Brevity

You should be as brief as you can without omitting any important details. About 95 per cent of people understand an eight-word sentence on first reading, but only about 4 per cent of people understand a 27-word sentence first time around, especially if it is poorly punctuated. In fact, the sentence you have just read contains 34 words, and presumably you found little trouble in reading it: this exemplifies the value of good punctuation in helping you get your message across.

Aim to convey only one thought, or point, in each sentence — but make sure that you do not end up with a whole string of very short sentences. This has a sort of staccato effect when your letter is being read, which can in itself be a barrier to good communication. Try to achieve a balance between shorter sentences and longer ones.

Each of your paragraphs should deal with a single topic. Once you have finished with that topic, start a new paragraph. Do not be inhibited about short paragraphs. You may have been told at school that single-sentence paragraphs are frowned upon, but your object is to convey information as accurately as possible. Conversely if a single topic is such that to discuss it in one paragraph would make for a dauntingly long paragraph, think of the topic as having subdivisions, and split the text up into two or more paragraphs accordingly. Never, though, end a paragraph just because it seems to be getting a bit long: unless your paragraph breaks come in logical places you are likely to confuse your reader.

Avoid unnecessary verbiage of the old-fashioned kind. Expressions such as 'it should be appreciated that' can almost always be deleted entirely without affecting the sense of what you are writing.

Clarity

Be as precise as you can be. If by an 'item of cutlery' you mean a knife, then write 'knife'. A 'large area' could mean anything from a big garden to the continent of Asia, so give the area in figures, even if the figures are only an estimate (in which case you should say so). Remember the comments in this connection when we were discussing how to write effective reports, in Chapter 5? Well, the same holds true here, only more so.

As in all the other areas of communication covered in this book, avoid jargon. Where you are forced to use some obscure piece of terminology, you may need to spell out exactly what it means; likewise for acronyms and abbreviations. Do not rely upon your reader having a full knowledge of 'business shorthand'. Use the correct terminology, because the reader's use of that piece of shorthand may very well differ subtly — or even not-so-subtly — from yours.

In some instances, brevity and clarity will make unhappy bedfellows, in which case brevity has to be sacrificed for the sake of clarity. Do not use this as an excuse to produce reams of tedious waffle, or to patronise your reader. However, if a longer explanation will make a point more accurately or more clearly, then by all means give one. You should provide enough information for your reader to understand your point, but not so much that the point is lost.

One final point on letter writing: It is often very tempting, when you are really furious about something, to write the stiffest letter of all time — a 'cardboard' letter, in fact. The best tip is: don't. If you can, put off writing the letter for a day or two. If you cannot, write the letter to get the wrath out of your system, tear it up, and then write the letter you ought to send. It is often very useful to ask the opinion of the secretary who has to type up your testament of fury. A good secretary will tell you to stop being so silly, and later you will be very grateful.

Communicating over the telephone

If you were to telephone ten organisations, how many would impress you with their good telephone practice?

- how long would it be before the operator answered?
- how would the operator answer?
- how long would it be before you were put through?
- would you be certain to be put through to the right person or department first time?
- would you be passed from pillar to post before getting the answer you wanted?
- would people call you back if they said they were going to?
- would it be a pleasure to deal with that company over the telephone, or would it be frustrating and time-wasting?

Now that you are smugly thinking of all the companies you know whose telephone practice is appalling, here is one final question for you:

- does your organisation pass the 'telephone test'?

It is quite likely that the honest answer is 'no'.

The telephone plays a vital part in any firm. Properly used, it is a major asset. Misused, it not only wastes time and money, it loses you business. So you must do everything in your power to ensure that your organisation uses the telephone efficiently and in a way that reflects well on the organisation. The extent to which you can do this probably depends on how far up the ladder you have climbed, but there is at least one part of the organisation whose telephone practice you can improve: you.

When we talk to people face to face we have the great advantage of being able to see them. We can take advantage of learning from their body language what they really mean, or whether they are understanding what we say to them. On the telephone, denied this channel of communication, we have instead to rely on only two things: words and tone of voice. This works both ways. We have to concentrate on the other person's speech, and we have to make sure that our own words and tone of voice are conveying what we want them to convey.

It is tempting to think that listening to someone on the telephone is a passive activity — unlike speaking to them. But this is not the case if you are listening *well*. Indeed, listening well is a much more demanding activity than speaking. There are many factors that cannot only stop you listening well but actually stop you really listening at all. You may have a preconceived idea of what the caller is going to say, or something interesting may be going on in the office, or the caller may simply have a boring voice. In any such instance, you must work extra hard to make sure you are listening properly.

To help you, it is a good idea to concentrate your mind on the subject by taking notes. Have a pad and a pen next to your telephone at all times, if necessary fixed to the desk in some way so that they do not get lost or filched. Scrabbling around for writing materials after the call has started is frustrating for you and does not create a good impression on the caller. Taking notes right from the start of the conversation also means that you do not have to go back and recap later. Of course, often enough you will simply throw away the notes after the conversation is over, but in some cases they will be of considerable use to you.

Good listening, just as when you are in a face-to-face encounter, also involves communicating to the caller that you are indeed listening. On the telephone you have to use, as it were, 'verbal nods'. Things like 'I see', 'yes', 'OK', 'right' and 'hmmm' all indicate to the caller that, yes, you are still there and, yes, you are still listening.

When you are, in your turn, speaking to your caller, you still have to try to convey all the information that would be present in your body language were this a face-to-face encounter. You have to do this through a combination of words and tone of voice.

Words are the tools of a speaker's trade, and you should use them carefully. Employ words that create a picture in the caller's mind: 'I'll just check that in the files — shouldn't be a minute' will keep the caller much happier than a stark, unexplained mutter of 'hold on'. Obviously, you should avoid jargon, but at the same time do not be too colloquial or too familiar: most people do not particularly resent being called 'guv' or 'ducks', but a significant minority do, and the vast majority of people do not like it very much. And make sure that the words you use convey general helpfulness. If you are genuinely too busy right at that moment, do not say so. Say instead that you will call the person back in half an hour once you have sorted out their problem or at least got all the relevant data to hand — and *then make sure you do so*.

Our tone of voice is our other tool in telephone communication. You may be being bored silly by the caller, but you should not allow this to creep into your voice. One good way to make sure that you sound right is to smile while you are talking. Smiling relaxes the vocal cords and has a dramatic effect on the voice, instantly making you sound more friendly and relaxed. If you are good at making light, off-the-cuff jokes, then do not be too afraid of doing so. They underscore the smile in conveying to the caller that you are pleased to be talking with them.

Answering the telephone

When you answer the telephone, bear in mind that it is not just you who are doing so: it is your whole organisation.

The only difference between a business call and chatting on

the telephone with a friend is that there is usually a specific purpose behind a business call. To achieve this purpose, there are three main areas that need consideration: preparing for the call, controlling it, and following up afterwards.

You might think that there is no way you can prepare for an unheralded incoming telephone call. In fact, what you must do is to prepare not just for one call but for *any* incoming call. You need a good knowledge of your organisation — its products and/or its services — and of your colleagues. Obviously this is difficult when you are new to a job, but you should make every effort to find out as soon as possible. For example, a writer recently called a large publishing company that had just taken over a smaller one. He wished to speak to one of the editors in the taken-over company, and was baffled to be told by the telephonist that she had never heard of it and that there was no one of the editor's name in her internal directory. This reflected badly on the company — management should have seen to it that the new telephonist was kept aware of the takeover — but equally it said little for the enterprise of the telephonist herself. Common gossip should have told her about the takeover, and certainly she should regularly have been querying those around her as to whether her directory really was up-to-date. Even though you are at a more senior level than that receptionist, you too should make sure that you know as much as possible about your organisation and that you have an up-to-date internal telephone directory to hand. Also by the telephone you should have writing materials, as we noted, and, if you are involved in informing customers about products and services, a complete set of the organisation's relevant brochures.

Even if you find that you are unprepared for one call, you should make sure that you are prepared for the next similar one. Obviously, the first time around you must transfer the call to someone who does know, but you should follow this up by asking them for the relevant information so that, next time, you can respond to the caller yourself.

Controlling calls is vital, and there are a number of golden rules that must be obeyed.

- Answer promptly. You know yourself how frustrating it is to hear the telephone ringing and ringing at the other end, with no one answering it. If the telephone on someone's desk rings and they are not there, answer it as quickly as you can. The caller would rather speak to the wrong person (who can always take a message) than to no one at all.

- Give a greeting. This should have the form of 'Good morning, accounts department, Lydia Darbyshire speaking'. The three elements of this greeting convey courtesy to the caller, confirm that he or she has the right department, and usually elicit from the caller the caller's own name. This last is useful, because thereafter you can intersperse the conversation with the caller's name — 'I'll see what I can do, Ms Knowles' — which adds to the general tone you wish to convey of friendly helpfulness.
- Think about the questions you ask the caller. If you ask a closed question (see page 99) you will get 'yes' or 'no' as a reply, which will hardly help the conversation to flourish. If you ask an open question, the conversation may flourish too much.
- Keep the caller informed. Do not just leave them hanging on: tell them what you are doing and, if it is going to be some while before you can sort their problem out, offer to call back.
- Never try to hold two conversations at once. Even if it is the managing director breathing down your neck, concentrate your full attention on the caller.
- Check all details, such as name and telephone number, by repeating them back to the caller.
- Summarise what action you or the caller, or both, will take as a result of the call, and set deadlines for when this action will be taken by: 'I'll make sure you have that by next Wednesday' sounds a lot better than 'You should have that sometime next week'. Of course, once you have set the deadline you have to stick to it — or, at the very least, to telephone the caller to explain why you have not been able to.

Another aspect of controlling calls is the matter of transferring them. Make sure you know how to, and tell the caller what you are doing, also giving the name and extension number of the relevant person so that, if the caller is cut off, he or she can ring directly through to the correct person. Once you have your colleague on the line, tell them who is calling and why before you transfer the call. If the person to whom you wish to transfer the call is unavailable, ask the caller if they would prefer to hold on or to leave a message with you so that the right person can call back. If the caller elects to hold on, go back to them every minute or so to tell them that you are still trying, and listen to what they say in case they wish to change their mind.

After any telephone call that you have dealt with yourself, there is the important business of following up as you promised you would. In particular, if you told the caller that someone else would ring them back, make sure that person does so. It is unfair, but callers who are not phoned back will think of you, not your colleague, as being the inefficient one.

The rules for receiving calls apply equally to making them, although of course it is much easier to prepare yourself in detail. Just as if you were about to write a letter, establish in your own mind the purpose of the call, and make notes about the various topics you wish to cover, to ensure that nothing is missed.

One further point about making calls is that you should think about their timing. First, telephone calls (at least in the UK) are cheaper in the afternoon, so, if you can wait until then, it makes obvious sense to do so. Secondly, lengthy calls just before five thirty are often not appreciated — especially on a Friday! Finally, if you are ringing someone abroad, take account of the time difference.

However, to reiterate, there is one crucial point about every telephone conversation you have: put everything else out of your mind and concentrate your attention entirely on the caller. In so doing, you can avoid conveying any negative emotions — boredom, harrassment or whatever — and can gain far more information from the call because you are listening more attentively to what the caller is trying to communicate to you. Never forget that communication is a two-way process, and the truly communicative manager is as eager to gain information as to convey it.

You may often think that your telephone is your enemy, especially when it rings while you are in the middle of doing something else. However, just think of all the times when your telephone has been your friend, and you will stop resenting its occasional inconvenient intrusions.

9 WORKING WITH YOUR SECRETARY

Far too many managers fail to realise that their secretaries are the most important element in the entire communication network — arguably more important than the managers themselves. It is your secretary who is, as it were, your channel of communication both to the outside world and within the organisation. If your secretary is good, then you come across to everyone else as being good. By contrast, if your secretary is lousy, then you can imagine what people think of you — and possibly quite rightly, because you have failed to develop your secretary. Of course, some people are pretty difficult to develop, but anyone who has learnt how to type and take shorthand efficiently is unlikely to be anybody's fool, so the problem probably lies with you or, conceivably, with an organisation that has failed to allow the facilities and/or time for you to develop your secretary, and your partnership with your secretary, effectively.

It is a curious irony that, while organisations are prepared to spend vast sums on training managers, they seem reluctant to do the same with the secretaries. Perhaps managers believe that 'common sense' (whatever that is) and 'inherent ability' are sufficient qualities to make a good partnership with their secretaries, but this is manifestly not the case: the overwhelming majority of secretaries leaving their jobs do so because they feel a lack of involvement.

If you think of your secretary as just a sort of shorthand-filing-and-typing machine, then you are allowing most of your efforts at communication to fall at the first hurdle. Your secretary is, in a way, your *alter ego*. In this chapter we shall look briefly at how working better with your secretary can improve your abilities to communicate what you want to communicate, both within the company and outside it.

Another point concerning secretaries and communication is this: if you cannot communicate effectively with your secretary, then how likely is it that you are communicating effectively with anyone else?

Although the number of male secretaries is increasing, the vast majority are female. We shall assume here that your secretary is female — not for sexist reasons but simply for the sake of brevity.

Partnership in the office

Anyone in a responsible post faces business life in partnership with his or her secretary. How effective the partnership is depends on many factors, but there can be little doubt that any time, thought and energy used on making it work is well rewarded. After all, your first priority is to organise your support services so that expended time and creative thought can together achieve the best results possible — in other words, to create productive time. Your secretary is one of the most important keys to your being able to do this.

Today, at all levels, managers are under ever-increasing pressure. Many of us have secretaries who are desperate to help relieve that pressure, but who are never given the opportunity to do so. It is paradoxical that so many able executives are hampered in their work because of the lack of good secretarial help while at the same time there are many able, keen and conscientious secretaries who drift from job to job seeking work that will give them some kind of satisfaction. Some of them, of course, eventually climb onto the managerial ladder; others are doomed to a working career of constant frustration because their bosses are too insensitive or too stupid to recognise that the only sensible way for manager and secretary to work together is as a partnership, as a team.

Secretaries often complain of overwork, but when they do so they rarely mean that they are having to work too hard: what they are saying is that they have too much drudgery and not enough involvement in their job. They recognise that, for a variety of reasons, their boss is making it impossible for them to do a job satisfying and worthwhile to themselves or anyone else.

You can see direct evidence of one of the greatest misconceptions many executives have about the role of the secretary simply by glancing at the 'sit. vac.' columns of the local press. All the advertisements seem to be aimed at the same secretary, who is expected to perform the same duties. Of course, this is nonsense: different jobs and different managers need different secretaries with different aptitudes and interests.

If the partnership is to work to the advantage of both members of the team, it is necessary that you and your secretary fully understand each other's role in it. Every secretarial job is different, because each of them depends not just on the demands of the job but also on the personalities of the two people involved. It is not at all uncommon for a manager who moves from one organisation to another to be followed or even accompanied by his or her secretary. This is not because of any emotional entanglement, as the sniggering canteen gossip would have it, but simply because the two people involved have developed as an effective team and, for that very reason, enjoy working together.

Starting work together

Imagine that you have just selected a new secretary. (You may have inherited one from your predecessor, but the comments below, with minor variations, still hold good.)

It is worth spending time on a proper induction programme. A good start will help your secretary to settle down in the organisation, grasp the needs of the job, and appreciate your personal likes and dislikes.

Together, you and your secretary should make a list of priority tasks and learn your way around the files. Either or both of you may want to make changes to the way in which the previous secretary ran things. Do not be dogmatic. Your secretary may have ideas that differ from yours and they are always worth serious consideration: after all, she is the person who is actually going to have to use the system, and she probably knows more about filing systems than you do.

Make arrangements for her to be trained to use all the office equipment, including word processors, computers, fax and telex machines, and even the photocopier. Some of these — especially word processors and computers — require some time before the secretary can not only master their use but also realise their potential uses, so be patient and allow the necessary time. Always remember that it is your secretary, not you, who will be doing most of the work on these machines, and that she will in due course probably become much more proficient than you in their use — so give her time to learn about them properly.

Your organisation may produce a manual that gives examples of standard forms for letters, reports and so on to be used within the organisation — in other words, there may be a house style. If so, you and your secretary are stuck with it. House styles of this kind are in fact a very poor idea, as they inhibit your freedom of expression. If both your secretary and yourself dislike the standard form, then there probably really is something wrong with it. If your organisation has no house style, or if you have persuaded the organisation to drop it, then work out with your secretary a consistent style with which you are both happy.

Discuss your secretary's job with her, but at the same time do not forget to discuss with her your own job. Remember, this is a partnership.

At the end of the first week or, perhaps, month check the secretary's reactions to the organisation, to the job, to your method of working, and above all to yourself. Make future dates in both of your diaries for meetings in which you can discuss working methods. Reviews like this provide excellent opportunities for frankness on both sides. Your secretary may be unaware of any shortcoming you perceive, and conversely you may be unaware of how some of your own working habits are making it difficult for your secretary to do her job properly.

Delegating

You should delegate to your secretary as much of the routine administration as you can, as well as whatever else springs to mind — especially some of the more interesting tasks. Managers are, rightly or wrongly, paid more than secretaries, and so obviously every hour that your secretary spends doing something that otherwise you would have done represents money saved. There really is almost no limit to what a good secretary can take over from you, provided that, where necessary, adequate training is given and that the secretary has the time.

That said, there are some basic routine tasks that you should not be doing if you have the support of a secretary. One of these is the keeping of the appointments diary. Far too many managers fall into the trap of keeping their own diaries and making their own appointments. Let your secretary control the 'master diary'; then you are free to attend meetings and so on secure in the knowledge that your secretary can tell people details of your whereabouts, time of return, and so forth. It is difficult for your secretary to feel in control of a situation if she has not been the person who initiated it — and it is hardly good PR if your secretary has to fob people off with 'I don't know where he/she is and I don't know when he/she will be back'. It is not fair on the secretary to have to be forced into making such responses.

A two-diary system can work just so long as each of you informs the other as soon as an appointment has been made. Otherwise, double-booking is inevitable.

Keeping your secretary in touch

Secretaries cannot do their jobs properly unless they have the answers to certain questions. These include:

- who is my boss dealing with?
- what organisations are we in contact with?
- what projects involve my boss at the moment?

You do not always have the time to explain everything to your secretary, and so you must make it possible for her to pick up as much as she can during the normal routine of the job. For example, if she opens the post and reads it before passing it on to you, she has a chance to pick up initial information, assess the partnership's workload, and be sufficiently well informed to be able to answer many of the queries that come her way.

Also, ask your secretary to answer as many letters as possible. Her use of English is quite probably better than your own. If a reply is too complicated to be delegated, so that you have to dictate it, encourage your secretary to be involved by asking her to gather the relevant files and papers to help you prepare your letter.

The telephone provides another good means of keeping your secretary informed. Ask yourself: What happens if I am not there to answer my telephone? The answer is obvious: your secretary would answer it for you. So why not let her do much of the answering for you even when you are at your desk? She is perfectly capable of answering most of the queries, and can put through to you only the most difficult ones, as well as those callers who really are better off speaking with you direct (for example, old customers). The more the secretary fields calls, the better informed she is of what is happening within the organisation.

However, getting your secretary to put through outgoing calls on your behalf is not a good idea: it is an old-fashioned notion that dates back to the time when all calls were put through a switchboard operator. The only instances when it is worthwhile are if a number is constantly busy, in which case it makes financial sense for your secretary's time rather than your own to be spent dialling and redialling, or if an overseas call has to be put through at a specified time.

Another area where you can delegate a great deal to your secretary is that of travel arrangements and meetings. Let your secretary organise these for you — after you have stated to her your full requirements. With luck, she will after a while be able to go ahead and set up exactly what you want without having to ask you first — this is the sort of initiative that must be encouraged. But it is important that you always give your secretary *all* the relevant facts, because she is otherwise likely, in all good faith, to make the wrong arrangements; for example, to buy a rail ticket, little realising that you have decided to travel by car.

Whatever the area of activity, do try to delegate as much as you possibly can. The areas we have discussed above are only the most elementary ones. Given a grounding in these, a good secretary will be able competently and calmly to take over more and more parts of your job, leaving you with extra time to do the things that you are being paid to do — for example, manage. Learn to trust your secretary, and offer her moral support by encouraging colleagues and clients to go to her first. Remember that you have two prime duties as a manager: to obtain the highest possible standards from everyone who reports to you, and to develop all your subordinates either for improved capability in their present job or for greater responsibility through promotion. Your secretary is almost certainly the most important of all your subordinates, and naturally you want the best from her. Also, although it used to be a truism that secretaries could be developed only to become better secretaries, there are now more and more examples of ex-secretaries in management positions.

So be kind to your secretary, and help her to develop. After all, she might one day be your boss!

Letter writing

Leaving aside matters of delegation, we have to remember that a considerable part of the time you spend with your secretary will be devoted to letter writing — specifically, you dictating letters to her. No matter how carefully you have prepared and composed your letter (see Chapter 8), all your effort will be wasted if the end product is tatty. Of course, if your secretary is a good one, you have no need to worry. She will make sure that the final result is well typed, attractively presented, and correctly spelled. However, it may be that you have to work with someone else's secretary or even with one of the typists in the pool. Obviously you cannot form the same sort of partnership with the typist as if she were your own secretary, but nevertheless you should try to inculcate the idea of teamwork. Establish who is the best and most intelligent of the typists, and try to insist that it is she who tackles all your letters. Agree with her the standard layout for your letters (assuming there is no house style) and discuss any other relevant points so that her terms of reference are quite clear.

Typing other people's letters can be a pretty tedious task. Any effort you make to involve the typist in what you are doing will help produce a better end product. Encourage the typist to feel that you are equal partners in a joint enterprise. Treat her as an ally, not as a servant. If you strike up a really good relationship, you may find that, as you are promoted, she becomes your full-time secretary — a boost for her and a delight for you, because your brand-new secretary will already be thoroughly attuned to working with you.

Dictating letters is something of an art. You should dictate reasonably slowly and at a constant speed, being careful to enunciate clearly. Give the secretary all the relevant papers, so that she does not constantly have to check back with you about the spelling of people's names and so on.

When you are dictating face-to-face, the secretary can of course interrupt if there is something she is uncertain about, but this is not the case if you are dictating into a machine. In the latter situation, try to solve all of the secretary's problems before they happen. Spell out any unusual words, give punctuation as you go along, and remember to give any overall instructions before rather than afterwards. If you say 'Please type that last paragraph in capitals' you are likely later to hear the sound of a typewriter being grievously assaulted, because of course the secretary has already typed the paragraph ... and not in capitals. Indicate the end of each letter you dictate onto the tape, and also always indicate the end of the day's dictation as otherwise letters may get missed out at the end.

Sharing a secretary

Nobody — least of all the secretary — much likes the situation in which two or more executives share a secretary. The whole set-up seems tailor-made for strife. For example, how is the secretary to decide, in moments of crisis, whose work is the more urgent? And whose fault will it be if she makes the wrong decision? Or even the correct decision, but one that is fiercely rejected by the executive whose work was put to one side? If secretaries are to be shared, then the managers involved must be particularly careful to ensure that there is no division of her loyalties and that she is never in a 'piggy in the middle' position. She must be encouraged, whenever she has received conflicting instructions, to speak to both of her managers immediately, so that they can sort out which piece of work is genuinely the more urgent.

Your responsibilities to your secretary

You must recognise four main areas of responsibility to your secretary.

First, you must communicate regularly with her. Check your diary against hers frequently, hold regular 'one to ones', discuss future plans and workloads, and in general make a point of constantly informing your secretary about what is going on. She is your main channel of communication, and she cannot communicate anything unless you have told her what she needs to know.

Second, make every effort to motivate your secretary. Encourage her at all stages, and make a point of giving praise where it is due. If you do not compliment her on a particularly good piece of work she will notice it, and resent the fact. Alternatively, if she has always worked for arrogant bosses before, she will be pleasantly surprised to find that you have noticed her good work, and will try to reach the same high standard more often.

Third, delegate as much as you can to her. We have discussed this topic at some length above, because it is very important. The more your secretary becomes your *alter ego,* the better she will be able to communicate the right information — and indeed the right image of you — to people both within and outwith your organisation.

Fourth, and last, a more technical point. You should have your secretary draw up her own job description, and make sure that you read it carefully and agree with it. From time to time, as your secretary takes on greater responsibility, this job description should be updated. It should be used at appraisal interviews, of course, but, much more important, it should be used by you as a tool whereby you can monitor your secretary's development and evaluate your own job description.

To sum up, your secretary is your most important line of communication. To look at it another way, as we have already noted, if you are failing to communicate effectively with your secretary, then it is likely that you are failing to communicate with anyone else.

CONCLUSION

As I wrote in the Introduction, systems of communication in organisations are only half the story, but a very important half. Team briefing and the methods of upward consultation advocated in this book are vital ingredients in any well run organisation today. But the other half of the story — equally important — consists of the skills of managers and supervisors as communicators. This book has aimed at covering both halves of the story.

Communication is not only a matter of action 'inside the egg'. The way that you communicate as a manager with those outside by telephone or letter, or in meetings of various kinds, could have an enormous impact on business performance. In other words, communication skills are an essential element in your overall effectiveness as a manager.

The result will be more than a free and accurate flow of instructions and information. A climate of good communication releases the creative or innovative ideas of everyone working in the organisation, as properly led quality circles have amply demonstrated. At the end of the day the tests of communication are:

- does the organisation achieve its common task?
- does it generate new products or services, or improvements in existing ones?
- does it create satisfied customers?
- does it grow high-performance teams?
- does each individual member feel fully involved and committed?

There is probably no manager in the world who cannot vastly improve his or her communication abilities by taking a little thought and by practice. May I remind you of my suggestion — if you have not done so already — that you read this book possibly a second time with paper and pencil at hand, noting down action points for yourself, for your department or section, and for the organisation as a whole. Resolve to review your progress at regular intervals. Many of the points in these chapters will have struck you as common sense. But you should ask yourself continually if they are common practice in your sphere of work. If not, then there is an agenda for action for you.

Lastly, as a leader it is part of your job to encourage and inspire the members of the team by your example and your words. You will not be able to do that unless you are first willing to listen to them. The ultimate test of the communicative manager is this ability to impart something of his or her own vision, sense of purpose and energy to others, as well as receiving ideas, suggestions and contributions from everyone in the team. The potential benefits to you and the organisation are immense. For, as John Buchan wrote, 'the test of leadership is not to put greatness into humanity but to elicit it, for the greatness is there already'.

APPENDIX: ORGANISATION COMMUNICATION PROFILE

Before introducing training for communication it is advisable to diagnose the training needs in your organisation as accurately as possible. There are several ways of doing this. One method is to gather together one or two groups composed of a cross-section of people at different levels and/or functions and give them a copy of the questionnaire shown in the following pages. (This questionnaire has been reproduced directly from a booklet called Organisation Communication Profile, published by the British Association for Commercial and Industrial Education.) The questionnaire has three sections:

- (a) a series of questions and statements which the respondent is required to read
- (b) a series of scales (the 'communications response') which the respondent completes having read the appropriate item in (a)
- (c) a 'master guide' for analysing completed questionnaires

Before a respondent is asked to fill in the questionnaire, he or she should be properly briefed. Here are a few notes on how to do this adequately:
- Explain the purpose of the whole work — namely, to improve communication within the organisation as a major contribution to overall effectiveness and efficiency. . .
- Explain the aim of this particular exercise — namely to diagnose and indicate accurately what are the strengths and weaknesses of the organisation as far as communication is concerned, and to gather their initial recommendations on what should be done, stressing the need for the exercise to culminate with a programme of action (assuming, of course, that the diagnosis indicates action).
- Describe the questionnaire as having sections, the first dealing with individual skills, the second concentrating on

125

communication within the organisation.
- Explain that information from the section on individual skills will be summarised in a collective profile but that the consultants responsible will be available to discuss the particular needs of individuals on a confidential basis.

THE COMMUNICATION QUESTIONNAIRE

Section One — Individual Skills

Your co-operation in completing this questionnaire in an objective and frank manner is critical to the success of this communication diagnosis. To assist this process we shall observe the following conventions:

- No individual response will be published or made known.
- All responses will be treated on a collective basis and only aggregate results published.
- Where specific comment or suggestion is of particular value, your permission will be sought before publication.
- The term 'Manager' used in the questionnaire, refers to all those who have a managerial responsibility in the organisation (e.g. including supervisors, unit engineers etc.).

The following questions should be answered by completing the relevant parts of the Communication Responses.

Personal Information

I   What is your job function?
II   How many months have you been in your present post?
III Who do you report to?
IV   How many people report to you (including secretarial)?
V   Is your job/work *mainly* concerned with technical matters? Or administrative matters?
VI   Do you have an appraisal system?
VII If so, are communication skills discussed at the appraisal interviews?

Skill Levels

This section is designed to provide a profile of you as a communicator. It therefore depends on your ability to assess yourself objectively, as you know more about yourself than any other person. You should have some *evidence* or data to support your response, i.e. feedback from other people — friends, boss, subordinates, colleagues, wife, children, etc.

A. Speaking

1   How would you rate yourself as a public speaker (i.e. before meetings of 5 or more) in the managerial contexts of your working life? (Tick scale).

2   How many times have you spoken for three minutes or more before 5 or more people at work in the *last month*? (The figure need only be approximate).

3   Do you feel that you are listened to sufficiently well when you want to be? (Tick scale).

4   How many managers in the organisation known to you would you rate as Very Good or Excellent speakers for each level indicated? (Tick box).

B. Listening

There is a difference between someone who merely hears what you say and someone who is a good listener.

5   How would you rate yourself as a listener in that sense? (Tick scale).

6   Again, how many managers in the organisation known to you would you rate as Very Good or Excellent listeners for each level indicated? (Tick box).

C. Writing

7   How would you rate yourself as a writer of memoranda or business reports based on feedback within the organisation? (Tick scale).

8   How often are memoranda, business reports, letters you write misunderstood?(Tick box).
9   A lot of written material generated within the organisation must land on your table. Please tick the phrases or adjectives which you feel best describe it in general for each level indicated.
10 What do you think of the overall standard of written communication within the organisation? (Tick scale).

D. Reading

11 Would you describe your ability to read a briefcase full of written material (memos, reports, books etc.) as rapidly as possible without losing full comprehension as — (Tick scale).
12 How many managers above you can read and fully understand what you write without further verbal explanation? (Tick box).
13 What books or magazines to do with your work as a manager or the particular business you are in, have you read within the past four weeks (excluding newspaper articles)?

Section Two — Organisational Issues

This section is designed to help us assess the effectiveness of communication within the organisation.

E. Downwards

14 How well does the organisation pass information downwards? (Tick scale).
15 How did you learn about the last piece of really significant news affecting the present position, profitability, employment or future prospects of the company? (This question should only be answered if the news was received within the last four months).
    A   From immediate boss
    B   By hearsay or grapevine
    C   In company newspaper

D   Letter or memo
E   At a large meeting (more than 50)
F   By closed circuit television
G   At a briefing group
H   In local or national newspaper
I   Television or radio   (Give appropriate letter)

16 By what route do you usually learn about important issues affecting you; the part of the organisation to which you belong; and the company? (Use the letter as above to indicate route).

17a Is there a system of group communication in your organisation?

17b If so, when did you last attend a group meeting?

18 How many were present?

19 Have you convened such a group yourself in the last six months?

20 Have you spoken to such a group in the last six months?

21 How many times?

22 How many were there?

23 What was the essential message you passed down at the last meeting?

24 Did you have a written brief?

25 Was this adequate?

Does the management above you satisfactorily pass down information about the following matters through *face-to-face* communication? (Tick appropriate box).

The Common Task

26 Purpose of organisation in society.

27 Aims and objectives of organisation as a whole.

28 Policies and policy changes.

29 Future prospects (the state of the order book etc.).

30 Achievements, results, progress.

31 Profits (the balance sheet explained).

Maintenance

32 Structural changes, reorganisation and the reasons for it.

33 Personnel and Relations at Work Policies.

Individual Needs

34 Pay and employment prospects.

35 Conditions of service.

36 Health and Safety measures.
37 Personal objectives and achievements.
38 Training and development possibilities.

F. Lateral

39 How do you assess lateral (i.e. sideways, on the same level) communications within the organisation as a whole? (Tick scale).

Rate the following factors as the causes of any breakdown in lateral communications you have experienced in the past six months.

40 Individual unaware of need to co-operate with others.
41 Too few meetings due to geographical distance.
42 Too few meetings owing to time pressures.
43 Poorly conducted meetings.
44 Too much departmental or divisional autonomy.
45 The centre is failing to co-ordinate the organisational parts.
46 Our size means we no longer know colleagues elsewhere personally.
47 Insufficient use of telephone, too much reliance on letters.
48a Any other factor.
48b From the above now choose three most common causes of breakdown. (Indicate by using number).
49 Can you outline one useful idea you have learnt from a colleague in the same functional area of the organisation as yourself but in a different location in the last six months?
50 The management group on your site includes men and women with different functions, areas of interest, professional skills etc. How often do they meet together in order to co-ordinate their work?

Tick the scale against the following statements about the management level or group with which you are involved.

51 (All of us share) a sense of common purpose is shared.
52 The particular contribution of each person is known and valued by the others.
53 Arguments about how one person's work fits in with another's are usually amicably solved.
54 Which functional group do you know least about?

G. Upwards

55 How would you rate the organisation in terms of its willingness to listen to ideas and suggestions, feedback and comments, passed upwards? (Tick scale).

56 Does the organisation have a system of consultative groups or committees for the upwards transmission of ideas about how the common task might be better achieved and how the organisation might work together more effectively and efficiently?

57 Have you led a meeting of such a group in the past (Tick box).

58 Outline one practical suggestion or idea about the task, technology or organisation you have received from below and seen implemented in the past six months.

59 Tick the box to indicate which of the following statements best typifies the way in which decisions are made in the organisation.
   (i)   They are announced with no reasons given.
   (ii) They are announced with explanations why.
   (iii) A tentative decision is announced; views are then sought before decision is confirmed.
   (iv) Several possible courses of action are canvassed before any decision is taken.
   (v)   People are fully involved at all stages of the decision; some sort of consensus is finally reached.

60 If you, or anyone else, has a good proposal which is being blocked by your immediate boss, is there any means of 'leapfrogging' him and presenting it higher up?

H. Auxiliary Communication

61 How would you rate your company magazine? (Tick appropriate square).

62 Briefly, how do you think it can be improved?

63 How often do you receive significant news first by the grapevine? (Tick scale).

64 Do all employees receive information about the company's annual results?

132

65 If so, is the information the same as the shareholder's Company Report?
66 Does it include more than financial information?
67 Is it explained verbally and discussed with all employees?
68 Can it be understood by most employees?
69 What else would you like to see in it?

I. Meetings

Taking an overall view of meetings you attend, indicate your own assessment. (Tick scale).
70 Effectiveness.
71 Variety of contributions.
72 Quality of contributions.
73 Time.

COMMUNICATION
RESPONSES

PERSONAL INFORMATION

I ....   II ....

III ....   IV ....

V ....   VI ....

VII ....

SECTION ONE – INDIVIDUAL SKILLS
SKILL LEVELS
A Speaking

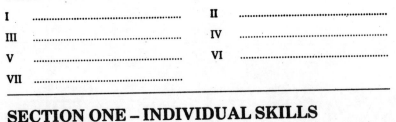

1

20	40	60	80	100
Poor	Average	Good	Very Good	Excellent

2 ....

3

| Never | Infrequently | Sometimes | Frequently | Always |

4

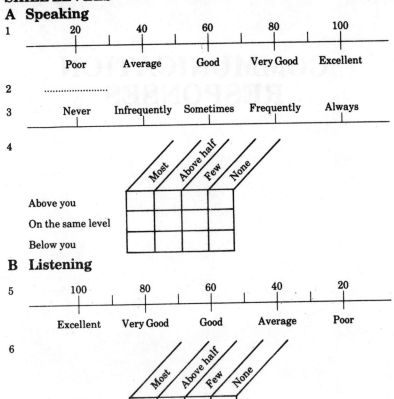

	Most	Above half	Few	None
Above you				
On the same level				
Below you				

B Listening

5

100	80	60	40	20
Excellent	Very Good	Good	Average	Poor

6

	Most	Above half	Few	None
Above you				
On the same level				
Below you				

C Writing

7
100	80	60	40	20
Excellent	Very Good	Good	Average	Poor

8
Never	Rarely	Occasionally	Frequently
☐	☐	☐	☐

9
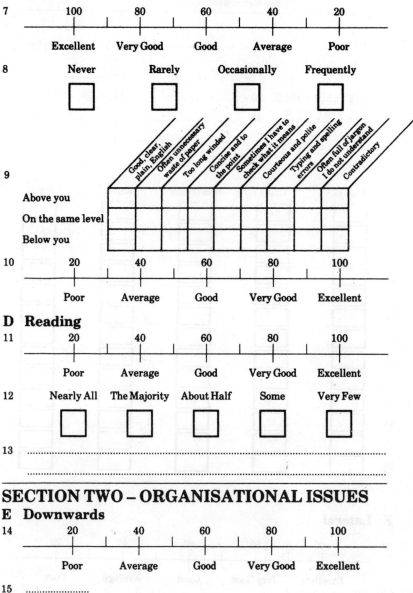

	Good, clear, plain, English	Often unnecessary waste of paper	Too long winded	Concise and to the point	Sometimes I have to check what it means	Courteous and polite	Typing and spelling errors	Often full of jargon I do not understand	Contradictory
Above you									
On the same level									
Below you									

10
20	40	60	80	100
Poor	Average	Good	Very Good	Excellent

D Reading

11
20	40	60	80	100
Poor	Average	Good	Very Good	Excellent

12
Nearly All	The Majority	About Half	Some	Very Few
☐	☐	☐	☐	☐

13 ....

SECTION TWO – ORGANISATIONAL ISSUES

E Downwards

14
20	40	60	80	100
Poor	Average	Good	Very Good	Excellent

15 ....

16 _____

Affecting me	The part of the organisation to which you belong	The Company

_____

_____

17a ....   17b ....   18 ....

19 ....   20 ....   21 ....

22 ....   23 ....

....

24 ....   25 ....

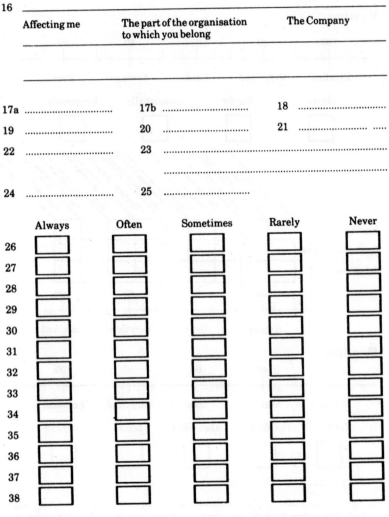

	Always	Often	Sometimes	Rarely	Never
26	☐	☐	☐	☐	☐
27	☐	☐	☐	☐	☐
28	☐	☐	☐	☐	☐
29	☐	☐	☐	☐	☐
30	☐	☐	☐	☐	☐
31	☐	☐	☐	☐	☐
32	☐	☐	☐	☐	☐
33	☐	☐	☐	☐	☐
34	☐	☐	☐	☐	☐
35	☐	☐	☐	☐	☐
36	☐	☐	☐	☐	☐
37	☐	☐	☐	☐	☐
38	☐	☐	☐	☐	☐

F Lateral

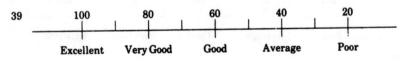

39   100   80   60   40   20

Excellent   Very Good   Good   Average   Poor

	Very Often	Frequently	Occasionally	Rarely
40	☐	☐	☐	☐
41	☐	☐	☐	☐
42	☐	☐	☐	☐
43	☐	☐	☐	☐
44	☐	☐	☐	☐
45	☐	☐	☐	☐
46	☐	☐	☐	☐
47	☐	☐	☐	☐

48a ....

48b ....

49 ....

....

....

50 At senior level ....   At middle level ....   At first level ....

	Substantially true	Only partly true	Not true
51	☐	☐	☐
52	☐	☐	☐
53	☐	☐	☐

54 ....

G Upwards

55

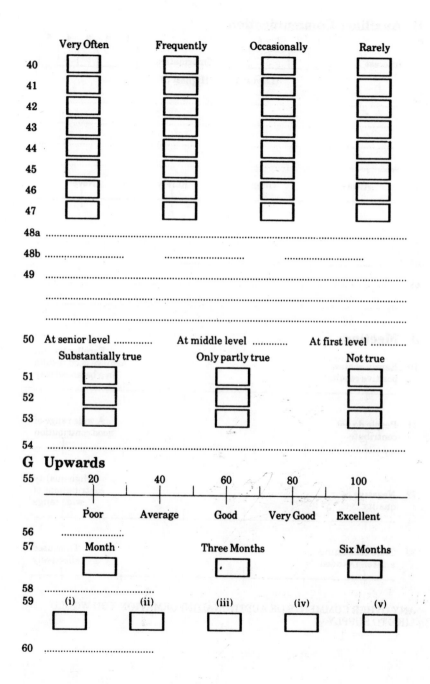

```
    20        40        60        80       100
 ┼────┼────┼────┼────┼────┼────┼────┼────┼
   Poor   Average    Good   Very Good  Excellent
```

56 ....

57   Month   Three Months   Six Months
     ☐   ☐   ☐

58 ....

59   (i)   (ii)   (iii)   (iv)   (v)
     ☐   ☐   ☐   ☐   ☐

60 ....

H Auxiliary Communication

61

	1	2	3	4	5			1	2	3	4	5

Interest   Information

(Lowest 1 – Highest 5)

62 ....

....

....

....

63   Always   Often   Rarely   Never

64 ....   65 ....   66 ....

67 ....   68 ....

69 ....

....

J Meetings

70 Rarely achieve
    positive results   Excellently run
                                            Achieve good results
                                            in a balanced way

71 People do not
    contribute   A wide range of
                                            good contribution

72 Negative poor
    quality   High quality
                                            contributions of
                                            wide range

73 Time consuming
    and long winded   Time used
                                            effectively

ANY OTHER COMMENTS OR ADDITIONAL INFORMATION YOU WOULD
LIKE TO SUPPLY.

TOWARDS A COMMUNICATION PROFILE

A Guide to Collating the Responses to the Communication Questionnaire

This guide is to help you to summarise and display the information recorded on the completed individual questionnaires (Communication Responses).

You will note that the Communication questionnaire response has a personal information introduction, followed by Section One — Individual Skills and Section Two — Organisational Issues.

Introduction — Personal Information
This is to allow you to analyse the responses under particular groupings, if you wish:

i.e.   Function, level in organisation, length of service, technical-admin, Managers-subordinates

It also indicates whether or not people are aware of an appraisal scheme and of being appraised for Communication Skills. The Analyst should place a tick (✔) against either the YES or NO for *each* response.

SECTION ONE
1 Profile of Individual Skills
You will note that these responses fall into two categories:

PERSONAL   — those based on the respondents' perception of their own *individual skills*

ORGANISATIONAL — those which relate to skills in the *Organisation* perceived by the respondent

In order to display the collective results, we provide scales etc. in a format similar to those used in the Quesionnaire and suggest

141

a single tick (✔) is used to record each response — giving a clear impression of the weight and distribution of the responses.
N.B. It is important to note that scales are occasionally reversed in the Questionnaire, i.e. low-left, low-right; in the Profiles we have kept to the usual convention of low on the left-hand.

An example of a completed scale, in which twenty managers and supervisors had taken part in the Questionnaire, might look as follows:

ILLUSTRATION ONLY

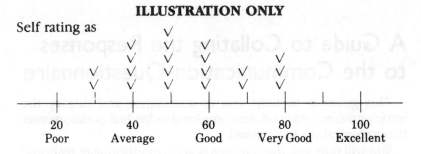

From the above you will note that we have gathered the responses into columns, keeping to the indicated measures and a point mid-way between. This depends upon the numbers involved and the spread of responses; the main aim is to display the responses clearly, in a way that can be easily understood.

All individual skills — SPEAKING — LISTENING — WRITING — READING — are analysed in SECTION ONE.

SECTION TWO
2 Profile of Organisation Communication Issues

In this section most of the responses are directly related to how communications are perceived by the respondent in the context of the Organisation and follow the concept of *flow* UPWARDS

↓ ← LATERAL →

DOWNWARDS

As most surveys will inclue various levels of Management, and possibly, people who are not, managers, it may be of value to separate the respondents when analysing the results. This can be done in various ways:
(A) Use two colours or more to indicate levels.
(B) Use an 'M' in place of a tick to indicate Management respondents.

(C) Have two separate Organisational Analyses, one for management — one for others.

(D) Use a code to indicate response, as suggested against Q.14. response.

Where YES......NO...... responses are indicated, as with 17a, it is probably easiest to put a row of ticks against the given answer, one for each respondent answer.

In Q.49. we suggest that the number of positive ideas mentioned by the respondent is recorded by a tick above the number given, this convention is used several times.

Conclusion

The purpose of these Communication Profiles is to bring the respondents' perceptions together in a way that can be clearly appreciated by those concerned with the diagnostic phase of any Communication improvement project, as a basis for improvement and development. From an initial analysis there may be indications of a need to illustrate results in a different way — either for more clarity, or because an alternative analysis may indicate the real nature of the issue concerned.

We shall be interested to hear of the ways you have analysed results and displayed the eventual summaries.

COMMUNICATION PROFILE

(Compiled from Individual Communication Questionnaire Responses)

		ANALYST
Introduction: Appraisal in Use:	YES	NO
Communication Skills Discussed:	YES	NO

Tick (√) for each response.

SECTION ONE – PROFILE OF INDIVIDUAL SKILLS

A Speaking   PERSONAL

Self rating as Public Speaker:

1

```
   20      40      60      80      100
  Poor  Average  Good  V.Good  Excellent
```

Spoken for 3 Minutes:

2

```
   1       5      10      15      20
           (Number of occasions)
```

Listened to:

3

```
   20              Sometimes         100
  Never   Freq   Sometimes  Freq.  Always
```

4.

	Most	Above Half	Few	None
Above				
Same Level				
Below				

ORGANISATION

Tick for each response.

Tick for each response.

Tick for each response.

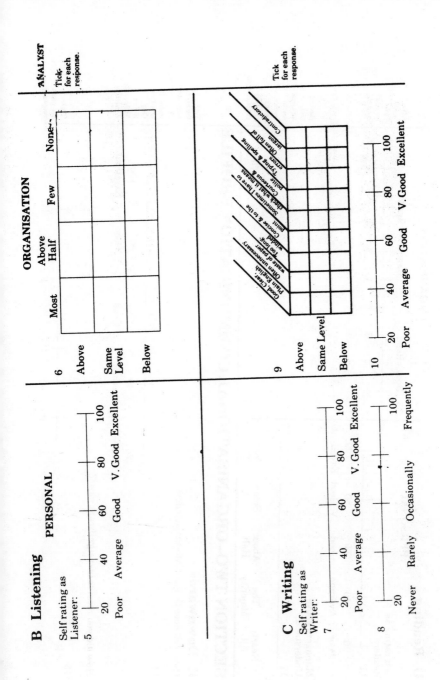

B Listening

PERSONAL

Self rating as Listener:

5

Poor	Average	Good	V. Good	Excellent
20	40	60	80	100

C Writing

Self rating as Writer:

7

Poor	Average	Good	V. Good	Excellent
20	40	60	80	100

8

Never	Rarely	Occasionally	Frequently
20			100

ORGANISATION

	Most	Above Half	Few	None
6 Above				
Same Level				
Below				

ANALYST

Tick for each response.

Good (Clear, Plain English)
Often unnecessary, waste of ...
Too long, wordy
Concise & to the point
Sometimes I have to phone
Courteous & polite
Typing & spelling often full of errors
Contradictory

	Poor	Average	Good	V. Good	Excellent
	20	40	60	80	100
9 Above					
Same Level					
10 Below					

Tick for each response.

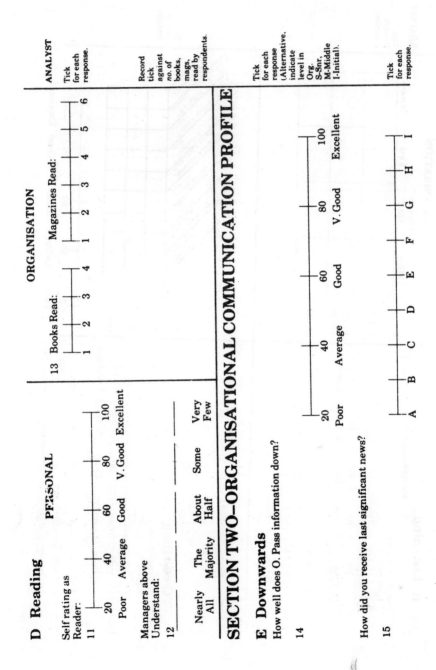

ANALYST

D Reading

PERSONAL

Self rating as
Reader:
11

20	40	60	80	100
Poor	Average	Good	V. Good	Excellent

Tick for each response.

Managers above
Understand:
12

Nearly All	The Majority	About Half	Some	Very Few

ORGANISATION

13 Books Read: Magazines Read:

| 1 | 2 | 3 | 4 | | 1 | 2 | 3 | 4 | 5 | 6 |

Record tick against no. of books, mags, read by respondents.

SECTION TWO—ORGANISATIONAL COMMUNICATION PROFILE

E Downwards

How well does O. Pass information down?
14

20	40	60	80	100
Poor	Average	Good	V. Good	Excellent

Tick for each response (Alternative. indicate level in Org. S-Snr, M-Middle I-Initial).

How did you receive last significant news?
15

| A | B | C | D | E | F | G | H | I |

Tick for each response.

16 By what route do you usually hear?

	A	B	C	D	E	F	G	H	I
Affecting me									
Organisation part to which I belong									
The Company									

Is there a system of group communication?

17 (a)   YES ——————— NO

If so, when last attended Group:

17 (b)   1 week   4 weeks   8 weeks   12 weeks   16 weeks

Number present:

18   2   10   20

Have you convened Group in last 6 months?

19   YES ——————— NO

Have you spoken to such Group?

20   YES ——————— NO

Number of times:

21 |— 1 — 2 — 3 — 4 — 5 — 6 — 7 — 8 — 9 — 10 — 11 — 12

Number present:

22 |— 2 — 5 — 10 — 15 — 20+

Subject of message:

23 | Health & Safety | Perform-ance | Business Results | Admin. | Technical | Budgets Finance | Organisation Change |

Written Brief?

24   YES —————— NO ——————

Was this adequate?

25   YES —————— NO ——————

Face to Face Communication (Do you receive information on the following in this way?)

	Always	Often	Sometimes	Rarely	Never
Common Task:					
26. Purpose of Organisation in Society					
27. Aim & Objectives of organisation as whole					
28. Policies & Policy Changes					
29. Future prospects (state of order book)					
30. Achievements, results, progress					
31. Profits (the balance sheet explained)					
Maintenance:					
32. Structural changes, reorganisation					
33. Personnel & Relations at Work Policies					
Individual Needs:					
34. Pay & Employment Prospects					
35. Conditions of Service					
36. Health & Safety Measures					
37. Personal Objectives & Achievements					
38. Training & Development Possibilities					

F Lateral

Assessment of lateral communication with organisation:

39

20	40	60	80	100	
Poor	Average	Good	V. Good	Excellent	

Rate following causes of lateral communication breakdown:

	Very Often	Frequently	Occasionally	Rarely

40. Individual measure of need to communicate
41. Too few meetings due to distance
42. Too few meetings due to time pressures
43. Poorly conducted meetings
44. Too much autonomy, division/department
45. Centre failing to co-ordinate parts
46. Size prevents 'knowing' colleagues
47. Too much reliance on letters

48(a) Any other factor:

Choose three most common from above:

48(b)

40	41	42	43	44	45	46	47

Useful idea from colleague in different location:

49

0	5	10	15	20

How often do different functions meet?

50 |—————|—————|—————|—————|
Daily   Weekly   Monthly   Quarterly   Less Frequently

	Substantially true	Only partly true	Not true
Sense of purpose shared: 51			
Cont. known and valued: 52			
Work arguments amicably solved: 53			

Tick responses.

Which function do you know least about?

54 |————|————|————|————|————|————|
Admin.   Finance   Mktg/Sales   Personnel   Engineering   Production   Quality Control

Tick responses.

G Upwards
Assessment of upwards communication:

55 |————|————|————|————|————|
 20   40   60   80   100
Poor   Average   Good   V. Good   Excellent

Tick responses.

Consultative Groups?

56   YES |————————————| NO

Tick responses.

Have you led Group in last:

57 1 month   3 months   6 months

Idea received and implemented:

58 |___|___|___|___|___|___|___|
    0   1   2   3   4   5   6   7

How decisions are made:

59 Announced,   Announced,   Views Sought,   Possible Courses   People Involved,
    No Reason   Reason Given   Decision   Canvassed Before   Consensus
                                 Confirmed   Decision   Arrived At

Can 'blocked' ideas be leap-frogged upwards?

60 YES ——————— NO

H Auxiliary Communications

Rate Company Magazine:

61 Interest: |_1_|_2_|_3_|_4_|_5_| Informative: |_1_|_2_|_3_|_4_|_5_|

How to improve:

62 |___|___|___|___|___|___|___|___|___|___|
    0   1   2   3   4   5   6   7   8   9   10

ANALYST

Tick responses.

Tick positive responses against no. of ideas indicated.

Tick/ responses.

Tick/ responses.

Lowest 1. Tick responses.

Tick against positive responses in terms of suggestion.

ANALYST

How often is news received by grapevine?

63

Always   Often   Rarely   Never

Tick/ response.

Do employees receive Company results?

64   YES   NO

Tick/ response.

Is this the same as Shareholders?

65   YES   NO

Tick/ response.

Does it include more than financial information?

66   YES   NO

Tick/ response.

Is it explained verbally to employees?

67   YES   NO

Tick/ response.

Can it be understood by most employees?

68   YES   NO

Tick/ response.

What else would you like to see in it?

69   0   1   2   3   4   5   6   7   8   9   10

Tick no. of positive responses.

I   Meetings

Assessment of meetings effectiveness:

70

Rarely achieve
positive results

| | | | | Excellently run
Achieve good
results in
balanced way |

Contributions:

71

People do not
contribute

A wide range of
good contributions

Quality of Contributions:

72

Negative, poor
quality

High quality
of wide range

Use of Time:

73

Time consuming,
long-winded

Time used
effectively

INDEX